Praise for *Understanding Ruptured Mother-Daughter Relationships: Guiding the Adult Daughter's Healing Journey through the Estrangement Energy Cycle*

"This book is simply outstanding. I am impressed with Khara Croswaite Brindle's thorough and engaging writing style, which provides insight and application for healing the wounds of maternal estrangement and difficult mother-daughter relationships. Croswaite Brindle shows passion in writing this book and uses a hope-filled approach to address a difficult topic. As a professional counselor specializing in relationships, I highly recommend *Understanding Ruptured Mother-Daughter Relationships* to mental healthcare providers and those desiring to experience hope and healing."

—Rebecca S. Trouse, MA, LPC, NCC, BCPCC

"*Understanding Ruptured Mother-Daughter Relationships* addresses the complex traumatic fallout when this primary relationship disintegrates. It maintains a delicate neutrality that allows for a range of outcomes including permanent estrangement and the path forward. This is a deeply insightful contribution to our understanding of these dynamics."

—Barbara Forgue, LPC, Center for Human Potential

T0049319

UNDERSTANDING RUPTURED MOTHER–DAUGHTER RELATIONSHIPS

Guiding the Adult Daughter's Healing Journey Through the Estrangement Energy Cycle

KHARA CROSWAITE BRINDLE
Croswaite Counseling, PLLC

ROWMAN & LITTLEFIELD
Lanham • Boulder • New York • London

Executive Acquisitions Editor: Mark Kerr
Assistant Acquisitions Editor: Sarah Rinehart
Sales and Marketing Inquiries: textbooks@rowman.com

Published by Rowman & Littlefield
An imprint of The Rowman & Littlefield Publishing Group, Inc.
4501 Forbes Boulevard, Suite 200, Lanham, Maryland 20706
www.rowman.com

86-90 Paul Street, London EC2A 4NE

British Library Cataloguing in Publication Information Available

Library of Congress Cataloging-in-Publication Data

Names: Brindle, Khara Croswaite, author.
Title: Understanding ruptured mother-daughter relationships : guiding the
    adult daughter's healing journey through the estrangement energy cycle /
    Khara Croswaite Brindle.
Description: Lanham : Rowman & Littlefield, [2023] | Includes
    bibliographical references and index.
Identifiers: LCCN 2023001861 (print) | LCCN 2023001862 (ebook) | ISBN
    9781538174029 (cloth ; alk. paper) | ISBN 9781538174036 (paperback ;
    alk. paper) | ISBN 9781538174043 (epub)
Subjects: LCSH: Parent and adult child—Psychology. | Mothers and
    daughters—Psychology. | Alienation (Social psychology)
Classification: LCC HQ755.86 .B755 2023 (print) | LCC HQ755.86 (ebook) |
    DDC 306.874—dc23/eng/20230118
LC record available at https://lccn.loc.gov/2023001861
LC ebook record available at https://lccn.loc.gov/2023001862

Thank you to the clients who've trusted me to sit alongside you through a significant and painful point in your lives.
To my mom, who continues to be one of my biggest supporters and shows me how the mother-daughter relationship can evolve.
For my sister, who is embracing her new role as a mother.
I'm excited to raise our daughters together.

Brief Contents

Contents

Introduction

Y ou need this book if you work with women. As a mental health professional, perhaps you've already noticed the significant number of women whom we serve in our profession who seek therapy for a variety of reasons, including trauma, anxiety, depression, and relationship challenges. The relationship with their parent can influence therapeutic goals and shape who they are as adults. Dr. Karyl McBride (2008) got our attention with her book, *Will I Ever Be Good Enough? Healing the Daughters of Narcissistic Mothers*. Women felt seen! Dr. McBride named the difficulties of the mother-daughter relationship, including conflict, control, and possible painful separation if repeated trauma or abuse are present. Finding it relatable, others have sought answers with Dr. Lindsay Gibson's (2015) book, *Adult Children of Emotionally Immature Parents: How to Heal from Distant, Rejecting, or Self-Involved Parents*. Dr. Gibson's work explored the possibility of adult children distancing from parents as well.

If parent–adult child relationship conflict is a concern for clients, how can clinicians feel prepared to address the possible treatment focus of estrangement in the therapeutic space? Specifically, the ruptured relationship between mothers and daughters? Depending on your client, the goal of therapy may land somewhere on the spectrum of repairing an estranged relationship with her mother versus finalizing parental estrangement and redefining herself as the result of that separation. Clinicians need to be equipped with tools to hold space for their clients in ways that are helpful and supportive to their estrangement process. This book serves that purpose by taking you on a journey through the *Estrangement Energy Cycle*, highlighting the various stages with captivating stories of nine brave women in therapy. Thanks to the perspective and added insight these clients provide, both mental health professionals and adult women will feel better equipped with the skills needed to tackle the emotional roller coaster that is *Estrangement Energy*.

Structure

This book will focus on identifying the estrangement cycle for clinical application with adult women as clients working with mental health professionals. This book will serve as a clinical tool to address the challenges of estrangement and adjustment needs of these clients within the spheres of personal identity, relationships, and grief and loss in order to promote personal growth and healing in the therapeutic space. The content of this book will engage readers by (1) introducing the *Estrangement Energy Cycle*, (2) illustrating different stages of estrangement through client stories, and (3) providing practical tools for mental health professionals to engage with clients wanting to do therapeutic work around estrangement within a supportive and nonjudgmental space.

Identity Protection

Although this book features client experiences with estrangement, I have omitted or changed identifying details including names to protect their identities. Any resemblance to actual persons, places, or events is purely coincidental. Many additional details have been altered, and some of the people described in this book are composites based on several different clients.

Author Experience

Understanding how common estrangement can be, I recognize how fortunate I am to not have an estranged relationship with any of my nuclear family members. I feel lucky because, in adulthood, we've moved closer together, residing in Colorado to raise daughters and granddaughters supported by loving, involved generations of women and men. Although my mother and I had our moments of conflict when I was a terrible teenager, she is one of my biggest supporters in adulthood, including being a reader and first editor of this book. Even though we aren't writing our story, she and I have had moments of deep conversation and connection over these pages, an experience I will remember fondly as part of our ever-evolving mother-daughter relationship.

I am, however, married into a family with multiple estrangements, which has contributed additional depth to my writing. I consider their experiences enlightening and vulnerable, affirming what clients have helped me see and understand about estrangement over the years. I've written this book in my first year of becoming a mother, an experience with timing that is not lost on me as I attempt to build the strongest, healthiest attachment I can in my infant daughter's first year of life. I felt these elements were important to disclose in full transparency on the difficult topic of estrangement. Although I don't have the lived experience of estrangement in my personal background, I have taken it upon myself professionally to speak for women who seek compassion and understanding from professionals and community members alike, to better understand their challenges and needs when navigating the immensely difficult and defining event of a mother–daughter relationship rupture.

Estrangement Defined

1

WHAT IS ESTRANGEMENT? Estrangement can be defined as no longer being on friendly terms, a loss of affection, and alienation. Some would describe it as the process of disconnecting from a familial relationship to the point of no contact. Others would say it involves a sense of betrayal. For many, it's the rupture of a relationship due to conflict that removes close connection. Estrangement can represent the disconnect between parents and adult children or siblings, and can even be modeled as an expected response to conflict from one generation to the next. This book is about mother-daughter relationship rupture and estrangement for adult women and their mothers. More important, it's about how mental health professionals can support their clients who are in the process of estrangement, through holding space for pain, questioning, grief and loss, and identity transformation.

Sheri McGregor (2016), author of *Done with the Crying: Help and Healing for Mothers of Estranged Adult Children*, reports that 9,000 parents have taken her survey on estrangement from their adult children, many of them mothers. She provides ideas for mothers to heal from the permanency of estrangement when reconciliation isn't an option. In *Rules of Estrangement*, Joshua Coleman (2021) explores how estrangement for parents of adult children is confusing and painful. He highlights that there are a variety of reasons that adult children stop contact, including mental illness, partners/spouses, abuse, grandchildren, and financial stress. Sharon Waters (2019), author of *Estrangement of Parents by Their Adult Children*, second edition, describes estrangement as an epidemic that doesn't discriminate against parents and adult children of all backgrounds. This increased frequency of estrangement has generated a series of books to help parents heal from this excruciating outcome or to coach them on how to reconcile with their adult children. What's missing is a book that speaks to the adult child's experience. To rectify this important perspective, we wish to focus on the daughters who choose to become estranged from their mothers.

Terms of Estrangement

Unfortunately, due to the judgment and stigma that come along with the status of estrangement, many adult children struggle to talk about it because they are, in fact, still trying to figure things out for themselves. In an *Ask Amy* column titled *Estrangement from Family Is Hard to Describe* (2022), an estranged adult asks how to respond to people who ask about her family. Amy suggests that the difficulty of describing the estrangement comes from the person still working through their choice. Is this disconnect permanent? Are they taking a break from talking to let things cool off? Is this cutting off of their parents resolving a conflict? Does separation feel like a better term for what's going on between them? For some clients, the simplest, shortest answer to the question about family feels best. They may describe the estrangement as "we had a falling-out and don't speak to each other anymore." Others may resort to saying that their parent has died in order to avoid further conversation on the matter.

The fact that estrangement is ongoing and never truly feels like there's completion or closure makes it difficult to describe to others. As one adult child estranged from their parents for the past three years shared, "it's still a rough topic to talk about." What they went on to explain is that, even several years later, talking about the estrangement can bring up feelings of grief and anger because of the unresolved conflict or trauma and resulting separation it represents.

Much like the parents who are estranged feel they cannot talk about the estrangement without some judgment of their parenting, adult children feel criticized for their choice to estrange, making it hard for them to talk about it as well—especially when we recognize that estrangement is a present, here-and-now experience that impacts holidays and family gatherings, or remains the dreaded topic of social interactions. One colleague summarized the difficulty of disclosing estrangement to others by naming how she's experienced responses of others attempting to rescue her, lecture her, or adopt the role of becoming her surrogate mother, none of which are helpful or empowering to women in an estrangement situation. She confirmed that estrangement never ends because there are triggers within family events and holidays to keep it fresh in one's mind that they are estranged.

Unlike other losses where we hope to find clarity, acceptance, and healing over time, it is less likely that estranged parents or adult children will feel this type of closure or inner peace regarding their relationship conflict. In fact, it's not uncommon for adult women who become estranged from their mothers to experience their own grief response, which can make them question if estrangement was the right choice. With time, they may begin to recognize that their grief response is showing up because of the *difficulty* of the choice to estrange and resulting feelings of loss that come with it, rather than grief serving as an indicator that they made the wrong choice to estrange. Kylie Agllias (2016, p. 1), author of *Family Estrangement: A Matter of Perspective*, acknowledges this difficulty by stating, "in some cases, estrangement is initiated as a survival mechanism—the estranger believes estrangement is their only chance of moving forward from hurt (and maybe abuse)."

Physical Versus Emotional Estrangement

One distinction Agllias (2016) names in her research on estrangement is that there are multiple types of estrangement within families. The one people think about most often is physical estrangement, defined as distance or a physical separation where the estranger (adult child) and estrangee (parent) have no contact or close proximity to one another. This could capture circumstances where the estranger declines to attend family gatherings or holidays, refuses requests to see the estrangee, omits their parent from updates on their change of address when moving, and remains hypervigilant to possible sightings to avoid undesirable run-ins with the estrangee. Emotional estrangement, on the other hand, describes a more subtle withdrawal from the relationship, perhaps under the guise of being overwhelmed, "swamped," or "too busy" to engage or remain in close contact. Agllias (2016) names emotional estrangement as a possible precursor to physical estrangement, where attempts to contact or connect become one-sided, the estranger appears aloof or withdrawn, and when invited to spend time, says things that are noncommittal like "maybe" or "we'll see." This may also lead to limiting a commitment such as claiming they have other plans afterward or stating that they can only stay for a certain amount of time before having to attend to something else.

One emotional estrangement example Agllias (2016) gives involves an adult child who goes off to college and realizes the differences between their upbringing and that of their friends, resulting in further distancing from their parents. Agllias (2016) reports survey respondents indicated a decline in meetings, phone calls, social engagement, and overall reachability in communication as measures of emotional estrangement. From examining these two types of estrangement, it would appear that emotional estrangement is a more passive act over time whereas physical estrangement can be seen as a more active decision based on the estranger taking action to indicate estrangement as the preferred choice to avoid further harm or pain. Agllias (2016) goes on to state that the majority of permanent estrangements have several cycles of estrangement and reconnection before the final estrangement decision is reached.

Family Frequency of Estrangement

It is not uncommon for there to be multiple generations of estrangement in one family system. McGregor (2016, p. 77) reflects, "in some families, perhaps estrangement is even learned." Several researchers and authors have named the experience of estrangement as having a ripple effect on multiple family members and generations. Agllias (2016) identifies one type of family estrangement as *inherited estrangement*. In this circumstance, certain family members have been estranged prior to the birth of the next generation, resulting in the newest generation having no contact with the estranged party. The estrangement is enforced by generations before them, preventing a relationship or familial connection between them and the estranged family member, oftentimes with the youngest generation failing to recognize the estranged family member(s) exist. Another type of family estrangement is one where allegiances are clearly defined. This represents an estrangement where family members feel they must pick sides, creating additional estrangements within the family based on those alliances. For example, if an adult daughter estranges from a sexually abusive uncle, family members may respond by aligning with her in a show of solidarity against the abuse, or could align with the uncle and deny her claims, depending on their own values, perspectives, and connections to both the adult daughter and uncle.

In addition to estrangement being in response to abuse or allegiances, we are discovering that there are generations who model estrangement as a response to conflict, normalizing it as a tool for future generations. A parent who is estranged from their sibling could model this response as an expected or even encouraged outcome between their adult children and the same or additional family members. For one individual I spoke with, there was estrangement across four generations of family members. In their family, it had been modeled for decades that family conflict was irreparable and thus estrangement was inevitable. In this particular family example, estrangement had occurred multiple times between several sets of family members, rippling out to negatively impact other family relationships before permanent estrangement over four generations was reached.

Sibling Estrangement

As we've come to acknowledge, estrangement is not just restricted to parent–adult child relationships; it can occur in extended family relationships and sibling relationships as well. As another example of estrangement modeling, there may be a sibling estrangement in the parents' generation where an adult child then sees estrangement as a possibility for themselves within a contentious sibling relationship because of that modeling. Sibling estrangement can look more like emotional estrangement, such as aligning with one parent or side of the family in a divorce and disconnecting with the other side over time through limited contact, conversations, or shared connections. Or it can look more like physical estrangement, such as cutting a sibling out of one's life, blocking their number, and forbidding them from visiting the family home because of their active addiction. Sibling estrangement can result from abuse or neglect, repeated emotional injury, substance use, or alignment with an unhealthy or abusive parent, which are just a few examples.

The Stigma of Estrangement

One shared concern for Coleman (2021), McGregor (2016), and Waters (2019), as authors of books supporting parents who've been estranged from their adult children, is that experts may blame the parents for the estrangement. McGregor (2016, p. 17) says, "after an estrangement, loving parents who did their best should not automatically be judged as uncaring, neglectful, or abusive." Coleman (2021, p. 1) sympathizes with parents within the introduction of his book, saying "[parents] fear someone saying, 'what did you do to your child? It must have been something terrible.'" Waters (2019, p. 49) worries about the long-term effects of estrangement on parents, stating "parents grapple with shame, self-doubt, and insecurity. Emotional wounds often give rise to physical symptoms and suicidal thoughts are common." Their concerns demonstrate a knee-jerk reaction within our community to assume the worst of parents, which is not the agenda of this book.

In her book, *Family Estrangement: A Matter of Perspective*, Agllias (2016) attempts to voice the experiences of both estranged parents and adult children. Agllias (2016, p. 1) recognizes the difficulty of honoring both sides by stating, "adult children are maligned for estranging an older parent, or parents are shamed for casting out a child, and other relationship types, such as sibling to sibling, are usually overlooked altogether." Agllias (2016) goes on to state that research indicates 1 in 12 people are estranged from a family member, which would imply that talking about it is necessary to challenge the former stigma of estrangement as a growing response to family conflict. Respecting that estrangement can be very stigmatizing and painful for both parents and adult children, I hope to provide clarity to parents who feel bewildered and blindsided by estrangement from their adult children and am tasked with speaking to the experiences of the daughters who have made the difficult decision to estrange.

Mother-Daughter Estrangement

The stories shared here represent adult women who made the difficult decision to be estranged from their mothers. Looking at the resources out there, what sources honor their process and reasons for estrangement, including respecting their refusal to reconcile if need be? Coleman (2021, p. 59) says, "for the same reasons that the mother-daughter dyad can be the most close and resilient of any family relation, it can also be the most fraught." Although each woman's reasons are unique, the women I've served for the last twelve years as a mental health therapist share stories of estrangement resulting from abuse, neglect, enmeshment, codependence, and trauma. As a professional helper, Karyl McBride (2008), author of *Will I Ever Be Good Enough? Healing the Daughters of Narcissistic Mothers*, had a similar experience in working with women. McBride (2008, p. 4) wrote, "I had treated scores of women who shared many of the same symptoms I was finally recognizing within myself: oversensitivity, indecisiveness, self-consciousness, lack of self-trust, inability to succeed in relationships, lack of confidence regardless of our accomplishments, and a general sense of insecurity."

Consider the following warning signs for an unhealthy dynamic within the mother-daughter relationship, while also recognizing that having one from the list isn't as concerning as having several warning signs, which increases the probability of a stressed or strained relationship. Grab the full checklist in Appendix A and download copies for your use with clients at estrangementenergycycle.com.

Warning Signs for Daughters

How would you respond to each question? *Never–Sometimes–Often–Always*

1. You agree to things for your mom that violate your own boundaries in order to avoid a conflict.
2. You feel responsible for your mother's happiness or mental health.
3. Your emotions are dismissed, minimized, or ignored by your mother.
4. You recall a childhood where your mother was absent.
5. You remember having to make your own food or attend to your own needs from a young age.
6. You feel like you make decisions about your life, career, or relationships to please your mom.
7. You feel emotionally drained after long visits with your mother.
8. When you see your mother's name on the caller ID, you feel anxiety or dread.
9. You are drawn to fun-loving or affectionate mom characters in movies.
10. You feel like your efforts are never good enough for your mom.

Warning Signs for Mothers

How would you respond to each question? *Never–Sometimes–Often–Always*

1. You frequently ask your daughter for help.

2. You expect your daughter to attend to your needs similar to a partner or spouse.
3. You have passed on anxieties and fears to your daughter.
4. You have shared intimate or personal details with your daughter as a confidante.
5. You worry that you are passing on negative patterns of behavior to your daughter.
6. You are concerned that you messed up or weren't around enough during your daughter's childhood.
7. You put relationships like a new dating partner as a higher priority than your daughter when she was a child.
8. You struggle with your emotions or mental health.
9. You struggle with substance use.
10. You feel detached and numb in your relationships, including your relationship with your daughter.

Women may be coming to therapy to work through the experiences listed above or to address the roller coaster of emotions that estrangement brings. They can have the desire to learn how to brave the cycle and implement new, healthy boundaries in having chosen estrangement from their mothers. Perhaps they are ready to embrace therapy as a space for re-mothering, which Karen C. L. Anderson (2018, p. 71), author of *Difficult Mothers, Adult Daughters*, describes as "feeling your feelings all the way through—of holding space for yourself in a way that, perhaps, your mother couldn't or wouldn't do."

Healing from mother-daughter conflict includes implementing healthy boundaries, which Alex Castro Croy (2022) sums up in his TEDx talk as #notmychicken. He goes on to describe how a lack of boundaries impacts a person's various spheres, including physical, emotional, relational, mental, and spiritual (PERMS). When we explore estrangement with a client through therapy, they can describe a variety of symptoms that show us just how much energy the decision to become estranged from their mother takes. It was something I began to recognize as a cycle of processing and healing for each woman—an experience I've come to call *Estrangement Energy*.

Take Nina, for example. Her estrangement energy showed up physically in her body as chronic pain. Not only did her back and joint pain amplify around trauma anniversaries involving her mother, through therapy she was able to identify guilt and shame as the sensation of tightness in her stomach, which sent her swinging between nausea and loss of appetite to binge eating and ulcers in an attempt to fill the void of the removed mother-daughter relationship.

Or Kathryn, whose estrangement from her mother showed up as anger to cover up years of emotional neglect. Kathryn found herself in midlife in escalated situations of anger, including road rage, yelling matches with her daughter, and altercations with her daughter's father. She would describe situations where she would go from zero to ten in anger, screaming at other drivers on the road or experiencing intense rumination on all the wrongdoings of her life. Each recounting of being wronged by others felt just as potent as the first experience, with Kathryn speaking through clenched teeth and tense shoulders as she recounted the week's events in therapy.

Relationally, Enid described her relationships as strained and superficial when starting therapy. She'd made the decision to keep her mother in her life after periods of disconnection and trauma, but found herself unable to relate to her mother at a deeper level due to her mother's ongoing addiction. This put strain on Enid's relationships with her sister and grandmother, who both had their own opinions about Enid's possible estrangement from her mother.

Mentally, Summer had created a pattern of avoidance from her mother. Recognizing her mother as an unhealthy person for her from a young age, Summer left home and found herself pregnant while still in high school. Summer was determined not to follow in her mother's footsteps, instead putting herself through college and graduate school while raising a daughter of her own. In therapy, she found herself shutting down when thinking about her mother's behavior over the years, consciously avoiding thinking of her, or changing topics when her mom came up. Summer's avoidance even manifested as her setting an expectation with her other family members not to tell her mother when Summer was in town.

Kasey's spirituality flourished in her recovery work. She found herself in the supportive circle of others seeking sobriety when her mother refused it for herself. Kasey recognized she had to grow up quickly to take care of herself when her mother drank too much and too often. When her mother died suddenly, Kasey's beliefs turned to questioning her worth in not being there for her mother through her own addiction. Through challenging therapeutic work, Kasey turned inward to her spiritual beliefs for guidance, and returned to her sober community for evidence of her worth to others.

Cultural Considerations

In focusing on adult women, a common thread we see for this population is the internal belief, "I'm not good enough." This belief can be seen in various women regardless of race, age, socioeconomic status, or sexual orientation. Additional cultural considerations can be organized according to the RESPECTFUL model from *Theories of Counseling and Psychotherapy: A Multicultural Perspective* (Ivey et al., 2001) defined as:

R-Religious and Spiritual identity
E-Economic class background
S-Sexual identity
P-Psychological maturity
E-Ethnic and racial identity
C-Chronological and developmental challenges
T-Trauma and threats to well-being
F-Family background and history
U-Unique physical characteristics
L-Location of residence and language differences.

Estrangement does not discriminate; however, it's important to explore similarities and differences for adult women who may choose estrangement from their mothers. **For religious or spiritual practice**, it's possible that women who have a strong faith identity would be at risk of increased guilt or shame for considering estrangement from their mothers. McBride (2008, p. 149) states, "guilt will rear its ugly head. Our culture teaches us that 'good girls don't hate their mothers,' so as you feel the anger, rage, and sadness, you can expect to feel guilt too." If their religious practice emphasizes the importance of family and honoring parents, estrangement can reinforce feelings of failure compared to others with intact family units, as with Toni's story, which begins in the next chapter.

When exploring **economic background**, it's important to recognize privilege where some women are fortunate to be financially stable enough on their own for estrangement to be an option. Estrangement may not be viewed as possible if feelings of financial obligation are present or when the relationship rupture would result in financial instability or uncertainty, such was the case in Kasey's story. As for **sexual identity**, gender in this book focuses on females. Sexual orientation can be a source of conflict in families where estrangement is then pursued in response to feelings of judgment or rejection, with ongoing research asking questions about bisexuality or homosexuality and elevated estrangement risks within families.

Psychological maturity can be viewed through the same lens as **trauma** and its potential to stunt emotional growth when experienced as severe or life-threatening in childhood. A question to ponder as professionals is whether there is a relationship between higher adverse childhood experiences (ACEs) scores and a lowered psychological maturity, such as we see in Regina's lived experience. **Ethnic and Racial identity** can serve to explore the impact of family values, such as the importance of family being reinforced for individuals who identify as Hispanic, Latino, Italian, or Greek, as was Nina's experience. Family importance can be seen in contrast to the American ideal of independence and self-sufficiency, which leads us to question, if the American ideal is independence from our families, does this somehow strengthen or validate the choice of estrangement?

Chronological challenges can capture the possibility of estrangement developing in adulthood. Childhood attachment requires connection to adults in order to meet children's needs so the choice to separate from an unhealthy or abusive parent isn't made by a child in this state of vulnerability. In fact, the opposite may be true. Young girls may overcompensate for the lack of healthy attachment by attempting to prove themselves as worthy to an aloof or absent parent. McBride (2008, p. 11) writes, "we daughters of narcissistic mothers believe we have to be there for them—and that it is our role to attend to their needs, feelings, and desires—even as young girls." The women featured in this book chose to consider estrangement in their teen or adult years when independence felt more possible or as the result of developing other relationships that could meet their unmet needs, as was Summer's experience.

Family background considerations capture the organization of the family unit. For some women, their estrangement from their mothers is the result of abuse within the nuclear family, as it was for Enid. For others, they were raised by extended family like Kathryn or by a single mother, as was Keisha's upbringing. **Unique physical characteristics** could lead to acceptance or rejection by a mother. McBride (2008, p. 7) writes, "a narcissistic mother sees her daughter, more than her son, as a reflection and extension of herself rather than as a separate person with her own identity." Should the mother's desire for a unified identity not be achieved, such as when a daughter seeks independence and distance in adolescence, the risk of conflict increases where relationship rupture may occur.

Lastly, **location of residence and language difference**s should be considered. Is the client an adult woman who is used to moving from place to place, such as being part of a military family? Have they felt displaced or have previous experiences of starting over, making estrangement and the resulting relationship disconnection feel less scary, as was Charlotte's experience? By using the RESPECTFUL model, we as professionals can take a deeper dive into the needs of our clients to show up supportive and empathetic as they navigate their own estrangement energy.

Clinical Considerations

In addition to being compassionate and empathetic, professionals have a responsibility to avoid doing harm to their clients. Lindsey Gibson (2015, p. 2), author of *Adult Children of Emotionally Immature Parents*, acknowledges that "among psychotherapists, it's been known that emotionally disengaging from toxic parents is the way to restore peace and self-sufficiency." We can't help but want to support our clients in cultivating healthy relationships in the name of boundaries. Coleman (2021, p. 29) pushes another perspective by asking, "do today's individual therapists increase the intensity and authority of the adult's complaints and raise the probability of estrangement?"

Surprisingly, Agllias's (2016) research indicates that professionals aren't directly asking about estrangement, which would challenge Coleman's claim. Agllias (2016) goes on to say that survey respondents report that asking about estrangement would actually make them feel validated and empowered. Not only would it normalize their experience to some degree; it would convey a professional willingness to be supportive while maintaining zero judgment. Additionally, it's our responsibility as mental health professionals to explore relationship dynamics as they relate to symptomology and clinical presentation. Asking about estrangement could influence and prioritize treatment goals related to self-esteem and healthy boundaries if clinically appropriate.

Contrary to Coleman's (2021) perspective that mental health therapists are encouraging client estrangement from their parents in pursuit of a client's desired independence and boundaries, it's more complicated than telling a client to cut off their parents. Nor should we give any advice or opinion on the matter as professionals. I was put to the test myself when a potential new client called me for a brief consult to see if we were a good fit for working together. She asked me what my views were on family estrangement due to abuse and asked if I believed reconciliation should be the goal. I recognized the anxiety in her voice with this question and knew she was asking out of worry that she would feel pushed into reconciling with someone who hurt her deeply. My response is the same as I would advise any other mental health professional: our clients are the sole decision makers in their relationships and lives, including the pursuit of estrangement or reconciliation. It is our job to support them with zero judgment and abundant compassion, whatever they decide.

Estrangement Explained

The professional empowerment of adult women may be one of the factors for why McGregor (2016) and Waters (2019) claim that parent–adult child estrangement is on the rise. The experience of estrangement could be more common now than for past generations, especially since Millennial and Gen-Z generations are participating in therapy to explore how to redefine their boundaries with their parents. Although both McGregor (2016) and Waters (2019) take a stance of supporting estranged parents due to them not always knowing the reasons for estrangement, this book illustrates the difficult relationship dynamics of nine women in therapy that led them to consider or seek estrangement from their mothers, most often due to significant trauma. Contrary to books out there, their experiences are not impulsive nor are they cold and manipulative for making this decision. As clinicians, it is our job to support our clients through their own process of relationship expectations, desires, and sometimes relationship ruptures that would lead to estrangement being considered. These nine brave clients will serve to illustrate parts of the estrangement cycle adult women can embark upon within the therapeutic space.

Long-Term Effects of Estrangement   2

C LIENTS MAY BE ENGAGING IN therapy for other goals besides estrangement, and yet a current estrangement status or the possibility of a relationship rupture between mother and daughter can have significant and long-lasting effects on women. In addition to exploring estrangement's impact from Castro Croy's (2022) PERMS model, experts have discovered that the grief and loss response to estrangement is similar to our anguish or pain response when someone we love dies. Agllias (2016, p. 53) recognizes that "estrangement is a particularly difficult loss to accept because it has no predetermined outcomes or end points." Within her research, Agllias (2016) describes a grief response to estrangement where a person is mourning someone as if they have died, which can feel painfully accurate when permanent estrangement occurs, eliminating reconciliation as an option.

Symptoms of Estrangement

Holding out hope for reconciliation and recurring feelings of loss are common for estranged parents, and yet adult children can also feel similarly. Even with personal agency to end a relationship through their choice to estrange, many adult children can't predict the significant reactions and emotions that will arise with their decision, feeling a sense of shock when they are fully immersed in it. They too struggle with loss and grief symptoms, some of which include

- sadness,
- anger,
- shock,

- helplessness,
- shame,
- guilt,
- loss of identity,
- feelings of blame,
- feelings of failure, and
- social avoidance.

The estranged daughter may report strain and mistrust in other relationships due to the circumstances of her estrangement. She may report difficulty trusting others or leaning significantly on her partner or nuclear family to prove that estrangement is not the fate of all her family relationships. She may report symptoms of anxiety or trauma responses, such as

- muscle tension,
- headaches,
- hypervigilance,
- sleep disturbance,
- difficulty controlling thoughts,
- avoidance,
- rumination on all that happened prior to estrangement, and
- flashbacks.

With prolonged symptoms and repeat triggers for grief, the stress of the mother-daughter relationship rupture can result in chronic stress symptoms for some women, including

- hair loss,
- weight gain,
- inflammation,
- moodiness,
- elevated cortisol levels,
- adrenal fatigue,
- thyroid conditions,
- sleep disruption,
- water retention,
- brain fog,
- headaches, and
- fatigue.

It's not hard to imagine how reporting these symptoms to a medical doctor could lead to a diagnosis of anxiety, depression, or posttraumatic stress disorder (PTSD). However, are we missing the mark in not asking about relationships and their contribution to a woman's symptoms? It could generate a clearer clinical picture to ask a female client (or any client for that matter) to describe their current relationships by asking questions like "What's your current relationship with your parents like? Who are you closest to in your family? Do you have any siblings? Are you in a romantic relationship right now? Who do you rely on for support?" By asking several questions about family dynamics and relationships, we can begin to explore the physical, emotional, and relational impact of estrangement on a woman's mental health presentation when starting therapy. This not only helps us begin to explore their coping skills as professionals; it provides us with a clearer conceptualization for their treatment plan and therapeutic goals, should they want to address the impact of estrangement on various aspects of their lives while in therapy.

Impact on Partners

Estrangement is so emotionally impactful that it creates a ripple effect on others in addition to the adult daughter and estranged parent. The partners of these women may feel the impact in watching their loved one go through grief and loss, anger, and oftentimes guilt and shame responses to the mother-daughter relationship rupture. Partners may feel they are walking on eggshells around their loved one due to the volatility of their emotions. They may feel like their loved one's therapist by serving as the sympathetic ear to the unloading of their partner's emotions about their estranged parent, and yet partners feel helpless to do anything to make it better. Without healthy boundaries, they may feel pulled into their loved one's grief while feeling their own mental health take a nosedive due to shouldering the emotional burden for both. Lastly, they may experience their own loss if they were close to or in good standing with the estranged parent, but now feel that they cannot have a relationship with them due to their loved one's choice to be estranged. In a desire for unity, they may feel they have to let go of the mothering relationship to support their partner's choice.

The impact on a partner was new for Keisha in her estrangement. When she and her partner learned that they were expecting a baby, Keisha's partner expressed disappointment that their child would not get to know Keisha's mother as a grandparent. Her partner joined her in a therapy session with her consent, in order to express his concern about childrearing and the impact of the estrangement on their child together. Keisha did the difficult work of holding space for her partner to better understand his concerns, in order to work together to find solutions they could both be happy with, especially since Keisha wasn't in a place to consider reconciliation with her mom.

Toni became more aware of the impact on her spouse (pronouns they/them) regarding her hot-and-cold relationship with her mom, Jan, after a series of stays in their home. Toni and her spouse felt the strain of having Jan in their shared space for months at a time. Jan's depression would cause things to fall apart, leading to evictions from apartments or loss of funding that would pay for her living situation, resulting in Toni feeling that she had to take her in. Jan was entering their home for the fourth time when Toni's spouse finally spoke candidly about how it made them feel. Toni found herself more motivated to create new boundaries in support of herself and her spouse in realizing that they felt as stressed out about the situation as she did.

If you are a partner to an adult child estranged from their parent, check out Chapter 17 to explore strategies that can help you and your loved one navigate their estrangement in healthy ways. If you are a clinician, it's possible a partner may disclose the burden they carry in individual or couples work, where exploring their needs in addition to their loved one's needs would be instrumental in maintaining their own mental health and well-being.

Impact on Siblings

The emotional and relational toll on siblings is just as heavy. Siblings feel they must pick sides, choosing either to align with the adult daughter or their estranged mother. This causes siblings to experience the loss of at least one loved one in the process of aligning with the other. Additionally, they may find it difficult to navigate holidays or social contact where the estranged party is aware of their time spent with an estranged family member. This might mean a mother who asks for information or updates on her estranged daughter. Or a daughter who makes seething comments about the mother to her brother, expecting him to agree with her thoughts and feelings. As we can imagine, this puts siblings in an uncomfortable position where they may wish to remain neutral, which takes work.

Kasey recognized the impact of her pending estrangement from her mother, Cindy, before she died, expressing empathy for her three siblings when processing things in therapy. She recalled how they voiced their frustration often, naming how difficult it was to invite Kasey and their mother to the same social events and keep everyone happy. Kasey watched in sadness as they began to choose sides, aligning with Cindy and accusing Kasey of being unreasonable and overly dramatic, attributing outcomes to her struggles with alcohol abuse.

Enid felt the steady support of her sister as she continued to evaluate her relationship with her mom, which only added to Enid's stress rather than alleviating it. She felt she had to make everyone happy, and was receiving more persistent demands from her grandma to cut ties with her mom. The more her sister tried to reassure her and demonstrate her love and support, the more Enid felt the stirrings of a panic attack in not wanting to disappoint her sister or her grandma with her decisions.

Striving for neutrality in an estranged family dynamic as a sibling can be difficult. Having healthy boundaries and redirecting criticism can help siblings avoid triangulation between an estranged mother and daughter. If you are a sibling struggling to navigate the emotional minefields of your relationships with your sister and mother, check out additional ideas in Chapter 17.

Impact on Children

Being an adult in a family with estranged loved ones feels challenging. Being a child witnessing that dynamic can be even more difficult. What does an adult woman say to her daughter who asks why she doesn't have a grandma? How do the adults in a child's life explain estrangement? What can be shared when a child comes home with a family tree assignment and asks why they don't have grandparents like other kids? How do we avoid parentifying a child by going too deep into the details of an adult estrangement? How does one navigate a child's irrational worry that they may be the cause of an estrangement?

Over the years, child therapists and grief experts have emphasized the importance of straightforward and truthful answers to children regarding all sorts of difficult topics, including death and suicide. When it comes to the emotionally charged topic of estrangement, the same rules can apply. You may have heard of the acronym KISS. In our example, KISS stands for *Keep It Short and Straightforward*. The length of the explanation is directly related to the child's age, meaning a short, simple answer for a young child and a potentially longer, more detailed explanation for a teenager who wants to know what happened. Straightforward is important to emphasize because it captures the importance of being honest in our disclosures as parents. Just as mental health professionals would dissuade a parent from encouraging a child to view death as "the person is just sleeping," to avoid or lie about a family estrangement could also backfire and have harmful consequences. What if your child grows up and realizes you kept secrets from them? Or believes you lied to them about the existence of an estranged family member? How would you repair their broken trust? The goal when a child asks why their parent doesn't speak to their grandparent(s), for example, is for the parent to provide a short, straightforward explanation that leaves the child with enough information to explain the disconnection without them feeling like they have to hold the parent's emotions in the estrangement or feel responsible for their parent's well-being.

Why are short explanations recommended? It's understandable that your child's questions about the estrangement can create anxiety for you. It's also not uncommon to overshare when feeling anxious. A great way to keep your anxiety in check is to take a breath and ask your child what they want to know about the estrangement. Their answer may surprise you! They may have a quick question that doesn't warrant significant anxiety, like asking where the person lives, if they look like anyone else in the family, or how old they are. Or they may want to know more about the conflict that led up to the estrangement, which would warrant a more detailed response. Even in this instance, taking a moment to pause allows you to remain mindful of what you share, keeping it focused on simple, straightforward details while grounding yourself in your emotions to avoid unintentionally oversharing with your child.

Below are some examples of possible responses parents can explore, in order to feel prepared for an inquiry by their child about estranged family members.

- Your grandma did some things that were very hurtful when I was a kid, and we don't talk anymore because of how painful it was.
- I've chosen not to speak to your uncle because his actions make me feel unsafe.
- Your grandpa is struggling to be healthy right now so it's best that we don't have any contact with him.

- Mommy had to make a difficult choice to stop speaking to auntie because of some really painful things that happened in the past.
- (For a teenager) I've chosen not to have a relationship with them and encourage you to explore for yourself if you want to have a relationship with them when you become an adult.

This last response is worth emphasizing because of the risks it poses to your relationship with your child should they develop a narrative of mistrust or believe you are trying to control their relationships. If your child finds out about a family member they've never met because of estrangement and they believe you've kept them from having a relationship with someone they assume would be beneficial to their life, their trust in you can be strained, if not broken. This is especially true for teenagers seeking autonomy in their decisions; your teen may be disappointed, frustrated, or angry that they didn't have the choice themselves to have a relationship with the estranged person.

Kathryn struggled to keep her temper in check around her daughter, especially when asked about visiting her grandma. Kathryn knew it was important to allow her teenager to forge her own relationships and make her own choices, and yet Kathryn struggled to be enthusiastic or joyful at the idea of her mother having a relationship with her daughter. She was feeling protective and threatened by the possibility that her adolescent daughter would choose a relationship with a grandma she barely knew over Kathryn as her mother, especially when Kathryn thought about their escalating arguments as her daughter hit her difficult teen years.

Summer focused her energy on encouraging her young daughter to develop meaningful, trusting relationships with her grandparents on her dad's side. Since there was no contact with Summer's mom, Cher, it felt relatively easy to avoid talking about Cher as the absent grandmother to her daughter. This dynamic suited Summer just fine in her desire to avoid all things related to her mom. Summer did, however, acknowledge her anger that resurfaced every time Cher missed her granddaughter's birthdays or other milestones over the years. Summer chose to see this lack of effort from Cher as confirmation that Summer made the right choice to break contact with her mom before her daughter was born.

Impact on Other Family Members

Perhaps you are a family member watching a mother-daughter estrangement take place. You feel loyal to both of them, wanting to respect their wishes while having quality relationships with each of them. This means navigating some awkward social situations such as holiday gatherings, alternating invitations to social events, or omitting that you saw daughter or mother when catching up or spending time with the other. For many family members, they feel they cannot speak of the estranged individual, much like some families work hard to avoid speaking of someone who has died. Just like when someone is deceased, the expectation is to avoid speaking their name or sharing anything about them, which weighs heavy on loved ones who feel like they can't share important memories because of other's discomfort. It's a mutual avoidance that has been reinforced by society, claiming that not talking about the estranged person prevents further hurt to the people they've left behind. For some it feels like an emotional minefield, requiring a delicate balance that each family figures out in the face of estrangement.

Nina's grandfather was no exception to the strain of estrangement. Serving as the patriarch of the family, he was respected and loved by several generations of family members who worked hard to please him. His status within the family was recognizable, as he was placed in the center of family events and was cared for by multiple family members as his health declined in old age. Nina recognized the effort her grandfather made to keep her in his life. When becoming estranged from her mother led to family gossip and sudden rejection, her grandfather increased his efforts to welcome her into family functions and into his home. The family felt they could not argue with him out of respect, and he did not tolerate their criticism of Nina, shutting down negative comments whenever he heard them. Nina loved and appreciated her grandfather dearly, feeling the loss of belonging within a family a second time, when she was no longer permitted at family functions after his death.

As a family member, if you feel like you are struggling to share your life without violating the trust of either party, you are not alone. You may feel like you are walking on eggshells or worry how they will react upon hearing the name of their estranged family member. It takes significant mental energy for family members to respect both an estranged daughter and mother in their lack of contact while maintaining connection through continued family ties. Check out Chapter 17 for additional ideas for how to maintain healthy relationships with both estranged mother and daughter.

Impact on Friends and Community Members

You may be a witness to the grief, shock, or outrage that accompanies estrangement for adult women and their mothers. You want to avoid doing further damage as you do your best to show your support. The ripple effect on you as a part of their community is measured in how their experience impacts your own narrative about estrangement. Do you feel reconciliation is most important? Does their estrangement feel abrupt, petty, or confusing to you? What can you say to an estranged daughter questioning if her mother should have contact with her children? Are you being a good friend if you suggest forgiveness? How do you show up when they share their moments of grief and loss with you?

Charlotte found herself befriending a social worker who lived in her neighborhood. When Charlotte received the first voicemail from her mother asking to reconnect, she went to her friend to talk about it. Charlotte was shocked by the vehemence that came with her friend's response. How could she believe her mom, Sandra, had changed? Was she that naive to think things would be different? What if Sandra hurt her kids? Her friend went on to warn her against talking to Sandra, believing Sandra's intentions to be insincere and manipulative. Charlotte left the conversation confused and in tears. She didn't know what to do.

Regina's faith community struggled with her estrangement from her mother. Several women in the congregation felt it was their duty to convince Regina to forgive her mother or risk living with significant regret. Others went so far as to warn her that she was disappointing God if she didn't reconcile with her mom. This wounded Regina deeply and activated a stubborn, teenage part of her within a trauma response. Instead of hearing what they had to say, she felt herself retreat into an argumentative, avoidant self. The more they pushed, the more she retreated into herself. This dynamic of unsolicited advice on reconciliation came with blatant disregard for Regina's trauma and abuse, preventing any kind of healing connection with other maternal figures, which was the one thing Regina desperately wanted from her community.

For many community members and friends, their own fears are activated when seeing someone experience estrangement from a parent. It's hard to remain neutral when you have your own thoughts and feelings about trauma, abuse, and the mother–daughter relationship. You don't have to risk making the same mistakes captured here when navigating estrangement with someone you care about. Check out Chapter 17 on the dos and don'ts for helping an adult woman who is estranged from her mother.

Assumptions About Estrangement   3

I N TAKING A CLOSER LOOK AT mother-daughter relationship rupture, we would be doing women a disservice if we didn't name and challenge the assumptions others make of estrangement. The community at large, as well as a handful of authors, have taken it upon themselves to be the voice of estranged parents everywhere. These parents, in an effort to understand the causes of their estrangement, report a number of similarities in their children that they feel contribute to why they have chosen to disconnect from their parents.

Selfishness

A leading critique in several books on the subject is that adult children who choose estrangement from their parents are selfish. They are accused of being self-centered, narcissistic, and focused only on themselves to a point where they disregard the hurt and pain their choices cause their parents. This may be true for certain individuals, but as this book will illustrate, women who choose estrangement from their mothers do so for a variety of reasons, none of which are solely selfish in nature. Rather, the choice to estrange comes from an effort to protect themselves and their partners and children from further pain or trauma from their mothers. Therefore, this difficult choice may be for the well-being of others in addition to themselves and doesn't omit them from their own grief and loss response when detaching from mother.

Summer was accused of being selfish and cruel for choosing estrangement from her mom by her younger sister, whose memories of mom looked completely different. It wasn't until her sister became an adult that she realized that Summer had made the choice to disconnect from their mother to protect herself from a life of small-town drug use and partying that would have held Summer back from her dreams of working with children.

Suddenness

Many parents of estranged adult children claim that the estrangement came on suddenly, usually without warning. Upon further reflection, parents are able to pinpoint signs that their sons and daughters were not happy with the relationship, but perhaps didn't feel it would result in estrangement. Although it may feel sudden, the process of deciding to estrange from mom takes significant time and energy for a daughter. Contrary to assumptions that choosing estrangement is easy for adult children, a daughter spends significant mental energy evaluating and reevaluating her options in not wanting to miss an opportunity to improve the situation.

Nina's estrangement from her mother was years in the making. After being subjected to repeated verbal abuse from a very young age, things escalated to a physical level in adulthood that left Nina with an assault charge. Even after serving her sentence, Nina questioned if estrangement was the right choice. She felt the loss of mom long before enforcing estrangement, but it took several years to feel at peace with her decision.

Therapist Recommendation

Another assumption named by various sources is that therapists are encouraging or championing estrangement for their adult clients. Oftentimes found in the same breath as the word "boundaries," parents and professionals alike feel that therapists are pushing an agenda for adult children to be estranged from their parents in response to trauma. As a mental health professional myself, I can see where certain clients may seek out advice or interpret a conversation about boundaries as permission to cut off a parent. However, a quality professional will remain neutral and help their client explore the implications of remaining in a relationship cycle that feels healthy or unhealthy, reaffirming that the client is the sole decision maker within their own life.

Enid admitted that she had worried that starting therapy would mean she would have to cut her mom out of her life. Several months into her therapeutic work, she reflected on how relieved she felt by the nonjudgmental, safe space therapy provided to explore her anxiety about her mom's addiction. She felt the therapy office offered a pressure-free zone—a place for curiosity that was a welcome respite from the urgency she felt from family members to make a decision about ongoing contact with her mom.

Exaggerated Trauma

Trauma remains a primary theme for exploration of estrangement. Several authors lament on how adult children may exaggerate their experiences of trauma to reinforce their decision to become estranged from their parents, to serve as a means to vilify and justify cutting off a parent. The challenge here is that society fails to recognize that trauma is defined by the person who experiences it. It is not our job to argue about what is and is not trauma. As you will see for the nine women found throughout this book, trauma is a relevant theme to why estrangement is considered. However, it is not the only reason, nor is it exaggerated to justify an action step. Instead, trauma work remains an appropriate modality in the therapy space in order to explore healing and goals for adult women seeking change in their lives.

Keisha felt like her trauma had been minimized for years by her mom, Jeanie. Refusing to put herself in Keisha's shoes, Jeanie denied that her violent actions toward Keisha were traumatic. Instead, Jeanie continued to justify her choice to put hands on Keisha, which was especially damaging to their relationship. Keisha came to therapy full of self-doubt about whether her experiences with her mom were traumatic in nature. It took several sessions for her to answer her own questions about trauma, in order to fully begin her own healing journey.

Refusal to Reconcile

Parents want to believe that reconciliation is an option, and yet for some, it will never be a choice. Rather than seeing this refusal to reconcile as a ploy for power and control by an adult child over their parent, it's important to explore the circumstances for when reconciliation isn't appropriate. For families damaged by repeated physical or sexual abuse, for example, reconciliation can feel like wishful thinking. How do we acknowledge the damage a mother-daughter relationship can suffer when subjected to repeated physical abuse? What supports reconciliation when a mom aligns with a boyfriend who is sexually assaulting her daughter? Each adult child's choice to reconcile or not is to be respected. To imply, as Waters (2019) does, that adult children are seeking apologies from parents as confirmation that their parents did something wrong in order to reinforce estrangement, is lacking insight into the circumstances that make reconciliation difficult to nearly impossible for some individuals.

Regina was one such individual who would not tolerate the suggestion that she reconcile with mom, not even when the recommendation came from her spouse or church community. Regina had done significant trauma therapy before coming to my office for ongoing support when her former therapist retired, and she made it clear that she knew her mother, stepfather, and brother's actions toward her fell under textbook definitions of physical and sexual abuse. She remained strong in her conviction to keep them all out of her life, instead seeking relationships with people who refrained from making assumptions about her family dynamics, including labeling their choices as mistakes that required forgiveness.

Too Much Toxic

Waters (2019) attributes the overuse of the word *toxic* to media and pop psychology. As it became more common in its application to relationships, this word has been seen alongside the words *estrangement* or *family estrangement* more often. Waters (2019) and others believe that adult children are using this word to justify their decision to estrange from their parents and to seek sympathy from others by painting themselves as victims—a viewpoint that only serves to discount the actual harm victims of abuse have suffered. Toxic as a word has encouraged folks to cleanse themselves of toxins, including unhealthy relationships.

What if describing a relationship as toxic is a means of simplifying something immensely confusing and painful—embodying an experience that we don't have the emotional energy or desire to explain to someone else because of the stigma, judgment, or emotions it stirs up when talking about it? Is it socially acceptable to describe a relationship rupture as toxic or simply state, "we had a falling-out," to serve as an indicator to move the conversation along to a safer topic? Estrangement is, after all, more complex than just saying "My mom and I don't talk right now. It's complicated." Maybe the toxicity we should be most concerned with is the attack on adult children who make the challenging choice to remove themselves from unhealthy relationships to preserve their mental health and well-being.

Kasey had learned to stop "cosigning other people's bullshit" in Alcoholics Anonymous as part of her recovery work. The word *toxic* had shown up frequently in the world of addiction, and in sobriety, she was considering its application to her deteriorating relationship with her mom, Cindy. The accusations and disrespect she'd experienced with her mother had escalated to Cindy threatening to show up at the family-owned townhouse to kick Kasey out. Kasey recognized that the growing sense of pending violence and hostility were putting her physical safety at risk, causing her to start looking for an escape plan from what she felt were toxic interactions, before things got further out of hand.

False Memories

A common disclosure found in interviews and surveys of estranged parents is that they have been accused by their adult children of neglect, abuse, or of being a bad parent. Additionally, parents can claim that their adult children possess false memories of abusive or unsafe situations that did not occur per the parent's recollection, leaving parents baffled and confused. Trauma has a way of being stored in people's memories in different ways with different things being the focus, which can mean one person's recollection can look completely different from another's. It's a similar phenomenon to why eyewitness testimony doesn't hold up well in court. You can interview three witnesses and get three completely different recollections of the events that took place. Parents are left feeling angry that their children are subscribing to false memories in order to validate their decision to separate or abandon a parent when, in actuality, an adult child's reports of mistreatment, however inaccurate to the parent, deserve curiosity and compassion if there is to be any hope of repairing the relationship.

In therapy, Charlotte recalled several times throughout her childhood where she had attempted to tell her mom, Sandra, about the sexual abuse by Sandra's boyfriend. Her mom rejected Charlotte's disclosures, stating she never left Charlotte alone with him and therefore Charlotte was lying and making up stories to intentionally hurt and upset her mom. What Sandra failed to realize was that her heavy drinking several times a week resulted in passing out for hours at a time, preventing her from protecting Charlotte from the sexual abuse that took place while Sandra was unconscious.

Mental Health Problems

Another common culprit in the blame-game of estrangement is mental health. The seeking of mental health diagnoses or labels placed on either the adult child or parent can be problematic and stigmatizing. In several books supporting estranged parents, authors argue that adult children may have undiagnosed mental health issues such as bipolar disorder that cause them to seek estrangement from their parents—which, as a mental health professional, feels like dangerous ground because of how simplified it sounds. It's possible that some adult children have mental health challenges or diagnoses that make them more likely to pursue estrangement. Equally possible, however, are times where a *parent's* mental health could be a factor in why estrangement is pursued when their children grow up. Perhaps it's severe depression or PTSD that prevents the parent from attaching or showing up consistently for their child. Or it could be a personality disorder, a topic McBride (2008) explores in depth for daughters with narcissistic mothers. By no means is mental health the only factor to consider in the research on estrangement, and if we are going to look at mental health within the family, it's best to look at the mental health of *both* adult children and their parents in our quest for answers on the growing rates of parent-adult child estrangement.

Toni had discovered the connection between her people-pleasing and her mom's chronic depression. Her mom, Jan, had suffered from severe depression symptoms for years, including during a significant chunk of Toni's childhood. This prevented a stable, loving relationship between the two of them, resulting in Toni receiving messages that she must earn her mom's love and affection by being a caregiver or helper to reduce or alleviate Jan's depression symptoms.

Control Over Grandchildren

An increasing concern for estranged parents is access to their grandchildren when their adult child chooses to estrange from them. One assumption we saw reinforced in several books on the subject was that adult children use grandchildren and withholding contact from those grandchildren as punishment for parents' poor choices. Although this is a possibility for some adult children who are angry about the estrangement and mistreatment they've felt they've received from their parents, the clients I've served over the years are more likely to limit contact between grandparents and their grandchildren when they are worried that the abuse or neglect they experienced in their own childhood could be repeated with their kids. In an effort to protect their children or to break an unhealthy relationship cycle, they may prevent contact between grandparents and grandchildren.

Kathyrn was struggling with her decision to limit contact between her teenage daughter and her mom. On one hand, she knew it was important to allow her daughter to cultivate relationships with family members unhindered by Kathryn's opinions or emotions. On the other hand, Kathryn believed her mom hadn't changed much over the years. She worried that her mom would unwittingly hurt her daughter by being a passive bystander to other people's mistreatment of her, much like Kathyrn's experience of her mom standing by as she experienced repeated verbal abuse by her grandfather. Kathryn wanted to protect her daughter from unhealthy interactions such as these, but didn't want her daughter to accuse her of sabotaging any potential for a healthy relationship with her grandma.

Assumptions of estrangement are widespread. This could be because of the emotional charge it leaves in both adult children and their parents, as well as the limited research to date that could shed light on why estrangement is being pursued more often in response to family conflict. As mental health professionals, it's important to be aware of these assumptions and any biases we bring into the therapy room due to our own lived experiences. By challenging these assumptions, we can find ourselves successfully providing a compassionate, judgment-free space for clients who wish to work through their estrangement energy and options.

A Woman's Worth   4

T HE SIGNIFICANCE OF THE mother-daughter bond has been written about for decades. Mary Ainsworth's Strange Situation was
conducted in the 1970s and explored attachment styles when
mom left and returned to the room where her baby remains with a
stranger present. Harlow's monkey experiments in the 1960s and 1970s
saw baby monkeys picking a furry surrogate monkey that could not feed
them over a wired, cold, monkey-shaped frame that could. From these
well-known studies, we understand that attachment is a bond forged
in comfort, security, and responsiveness in the mother. When healthy
attachment is absent, we see disorganized attachment, passive or absent
parenting, and mental health challenges in both mother and child.

Mother–Child Attachment

Recall the Russian orphanages (Merz & McCall, 2010), where babies
were neither held nor comforted. Instead they were reported to be in
their cribs unattended for hours at a time, receiving a message that they
could not rely on others to meet their needs and were forced to discover
ways to self-soothe instead. This critical window of development where
attachment to a healthy, loving caregiver was absent resulted in a series
of children being diagnosed with reactive attachment disorder (RAD).
Clinicians who work with individuals with a RAD diagnosis hear from
adoptive parents that the child has limited or no empathy, fights for or
steals the things they want without caring about the impact on others,
and reflected on how the child's behavior conveyed a message that they
didn't want or need anyone's help or love. Both child and adoptive

parent are blameless for these interactions. After all, these children have been in survival mode for so long.

In contrast, if mother can consistently respond to her infant's cries with comfort and responsiveness to ease their distress, the attachment bond is said to strengthen. Society encourages mother-daughter bonding through celebrations of its strength, its sweetness, and its importance in shaping daughters as the next generation of wives, lovers, and mothers. Traits are passed on, behaviors are encouraged, and personalities are formed. Consider the Enneagram Personality Test when thinking of measurable personality traits. As one of the more popular personality tests found both in the workplace and in dating profiles, would it surprise you to test a group of women and see several of them gravitating toward the Enneagram Type 2 personality—the Helper? Since caregiving is highly encouraged in our society for females, women may find themselves in roles of helpers such as teachers, nurses, and therapists. Or they may show up as a helper within their family system. In *The Road Back to You* (2016), author Ian Morgan Cron goes so far as to emphasize the importance of knowing our edges, which for Type 2s includes the "need to be needed." In an enmeshed or codependent relationship with mother, this can lead to women seeking out therapy in feeling burnt out, resentful, and anxious about disappointing others, including their mom.

Take Toni's burnout, for example. Toni had struggled with boundaries with her mother for all of her adult life. Depressive episodes often left Toni's mother, Jan, in hypersomnia that would stop her functioning, oftentimes resulting in her being evicted from her housing and living with Toni until she could get back on her feet again. Toni came to therapy to address her people-pleasing and perfectionism, uncovering a link to feelings of helplessness regarding Jan's recurring mental illness. Toni discovered her desire to become a medical professional stemmed from wanting to be an effective helper to others when she felt burnt out, ineffective, and resentful of the patterns with Jan.

Partner Attachment

Patterns of attachment with our mothers shape our romantic relationships as adults as well. According to Amir Levine (2012), author of *Attached*, the three adult attachment styles are Secure, Anxious, and Avoidant.

Secure Attachment is our ideal attachment type, embodying reassurance, safety, connection, and healthy communication with our romantic partner. Folks with secure attachment are paired up quickly and often because of their value to partners in how they make us feel safe and appreciated within the relationship.

Anxious Attachment describes a dynamic of insecurity and self-doubt, along with questioning of the validity of the relationship, our self-worth, and worthiness to our partner to the point of acting out from intense anxiety.

Avoidant Attachment describes a disconnected style where a person may state they don't want or need anyone, therefore responding with avoidance when pursued romantically. This response is most likely because they've become self-reliant due to being hurt by others in the past.

Stan Tatkin (2012), author of *Wired for Love*, describes the three attachment styles with a nautical theme that I think captures them easily for folks to explore in greater depth. Tatkin describes Secure Attachment as an anchor, Anxious Attachment as an ocean wave, and Avoidant Attachment as an island. Women I've served in therapy tend to identify most with the Anxious Attachment style, especially if mom was inconsistent in her care or responsiveness to their needs when they were children.

Colleague and fellow mental health professional Dan McMillan (2022) provides a relatable illustration in his animated video titled *The Badger and the Turtle: A Story to Help Your Relationship*. In this video, McMillan starts with an overview of attachment and then shares a story of a badger and a turtle. As they move through the world of stress, the turtle retreats into its shell, leaving the badger digging to get closer to him. As things get more and more stressful, the turtle retreats further into his shell, leaving his partner, the badger, frantically trying to get closer. This speaks to a dynamic of attachment we see in couples where the partner who identifies with the turtle has a withdrawal response to conflict or stress, retreating into themselves, which echoes Avoidant Attachment. This response activates their partner's Anxious Attachment, represented by the badger character. Relationship attachment can continue in this cycle without awareness, intentional changes in communication, and professional support to create a new pattern of connecting with our partners.

Keisha struggled with a hot-and-cold relationship with her boyfriend, even when he wasn't drinking several nights a week. When she would attempt to connect with him, his avoidant attachment response would result in further emotional and physical distance between them. This distance would activate Keisha's anxious attachment, causing her to pursue him, which manifested in demands and attempts to control the situation and him. Instead of supporting connection, her anxious pursuit pushed her boyfriend further into his shell. This resulted in anxiety attacks for Keisha, similar to how she'd feel when her mom kicked her out of the house for her chosen time with a new dating partner or boyfriend.

Attachment Trauma

Attachment trauma like Keisha's is a common theme I've witnessed in my work with various adult women in therapy. I've sat across from women who've expressed how they wanted to believe that they deserved to be loved unconditionally by their mothers. They desperately wanted the support, love, and protection of their mothers when they were young, and continued to question why they weren't "good enough" to earn love and safety when they needed it most. As we can imagine, this can contribute to the Type 2 Helpers of the Enneagram, with women seeking to be the most helpful or thoughtful of others to earn the love, affection, or admiration they've missed in childhood. Gibson (2015) describes this type of person seeking love and affection in adulthood through people-pleasing as an *Internalizer*. Internalizers put the needs of others before their own and seek validation from outside sources. This can be especially damaging when paired with emotionally detached mothers or mothers who are the perpetrators of abuse.

Keisha recalls how her mom felt threatened by her when Keisha became a teenager. Her mom, Jeanie, would demand that Keisha leave the house when Jeanie's boyfriend came over, fearing that Keisha would attempt to seduce him and take him away from her. When Keisha returned home early one evening, not realizing Jeanie's boyfriend was still within the house, Jeanie physically assaulted her, pushing her into a wall and threatening her.

Regina knows all too well what violence feels like in her family home. She described cutting off ties with her mother and siblings after her stepfather repeatedly beat her for not completing tasks around the house. Regina felt ganged up on by her mother and stepfather, recalling how her mother would stand behind him, watching as he struck Regina with various objects as he accused her of laziness.

Abuse

Significant or repeated abuse may increase the likelihood of estrangement in adulthood. Agllias (2016) identified how abuse situations can contribute to a child's feelings of instability within the home, including lack of safety and messages that indicate devaluing their role within the family system. There are five types of abuse to remain aware of as mental health professionals working with clients who are considering estrangement:

- physical abuse,
- sexual abuse,
- verbal abuse,
- emotional abuse, and
- financial abuse.

Physical abuse includes acts of violence or discipline that cause physical harm, such as hitting, kicking, pinching, pushing, slapping, grabbing, punching, or throwing objects at another person. There is a real possibility of leaving a mark from these acts, in addition to delivering messages of low value and self-worth for the recipient. Keisha and Regina both identified as survivors of physical abuse, with Regina being subjected to repeated physical abuse by both her stepfather and brother, whereas Keisha experienced physical assault by her mom on several occasions.

Sexual abuse involves unwanted sexual contact, oftentimes with perpetrators using force, manipulation, or threats against individuals who do not or cannot give consent. This can include touching, penetration, and intercourse that is not consensual. Regina, Charlotte, and Enid had lived experience with unwanted sexual contact. Enid had been molested as a child by a family member, Charlotte had been assaulted by her mother's boyfriend as a young girl, and Regina was sexually assaulted by her brother and his friends at a critical and vulnerable time in her life.

Verbal abuse describes weaponized words that are repetitive, cruel, and critical in nature. This can include insults, ridicule, humiliation, and put-downs that are meant to hurt or create negative beliefs and experiences for the targeted individual. Nina and Kathryn identify with this type of abuse. Nina was subjected to years of verbal abuse by her mother, who felt Nina wasn't meeting her expectations physically or behaviorally, resulting in verbal attacks on Nina's appearance, mental health, and overall existence within the family. Kathyrn experienced verbal abuse by her grandfather, who targeted her in his moments of rage within the household.

Emotional abuse comes in a variety of forms, making it the most difficult to hold perpetrators accountable for because of discrepancies in how it can be measured. Emotional abuse embodies a series of words or behaviors that are meant to coerce, manipulate, or exercise power and control over another person. This could include gaslighting, minimizing, and scapegoating, which are topics that we explore further within Chapter 6, "Cycle of Abuse."

Financial abuse has been added to the list of abuse types because of the equally emotional and physical toll it can take on the victim. Financial abuse describes the withholding of finances, limiting the victim's ability to access funds, concealing money or assets, or demanding paychecks be turned over to the perpetrator due to their desire to maintain control over money and thus the person. Often seen in domestic violence situations, a withholding of funds prevents the victim from accessing resources that could help them leave the abusive situation, similar to Kasey's situation, effectively trapping them in a cycle of power and control.

Neglect

Whether physical or emotional, neglect can contribute to avoidant attachment in childhood and an increased possibility of estrangement in adulthood. Physical neglect describes a parent who is absent from the home, such as one who abuses substances, a parent who pursues a new partner while leaving their kids at home by themselves, a parent who is incapacitated by chronic pain or frequent migraines, or a parent who had to work multiple jobs to put food on the table, as several examples.

Emotional neglect can describe a parent who is suffering from serious mental illness such as chronic depression or crippling anxiety that prevents them from being present and attuned to their children's needs. It can also represent a parent who is emotionally detached from their children, such as a mother who suffers from postpartum depression or a parent whose own trauma prevents healthy attachment due to them operating out of survival mode or having unmet needs of their own. The lack of meaningful connection can contribute to an adult child describing a childhood that was lonely, uncertain, and painful, making estrangement that much more possible due to them reporting detachment and distance from their parent(s) for years prior to enforcing estrangement.

Adverse Childhood Experiences (ACEs)

In recognizing the mental and physical impact of abuse and neglect, it's also important to acknowledge the long-term effects of trauma on children. The adverse childhood experiences (ACEs) study shed light on the significance of trauma and adversity within a family system, including its impact on children who developed greater risks for physical and mental health concerns as they aged. In a 2021 study conducted by the Centers for Disease Control and Prevention (CDC), a relationship was identified between events that challenged a child's sense of safety, stability, and bonding from birth to seventeen years of age, and the eventual development of chronic health conditions and increased mental illness that followed them into adulthood.

Examples of events that would be categorized as an ACE include (Croswaite Brindle, 2021)

- experiencing violence, abuse, or neglect;
- witnessing violence in the home or community;
- having a family member attempt or die by suicide;
- substance misuse;
- mental health problems; and
- instability due to parental separation or household members being in jail or prison.

While the number of adults reporting that they've experienced one or more ACEs in their childhood is growing, it's important to remain mindful of the possible connection between negative childhood experiences and eventual estrangement. Clients could come to mental health professionals seeking trauma therapy and healing for events that have happened to them, with or without awareness of how unresolved childhood trauma could increase the likelihood of a possible adult estrangement.

Although not all estrangement stories involve trauma, abuse, and neglect, the women featured here have experienced things that were manipulative, hurtful, and violent to the point where estrangement was something they considered to keep themselves safe physically and emotionally. Some were estranged prior to engaging in therapy, whereas others explored the implications of estrangement in the safe space of the therapy office. None of their decisions were easy, as you will soon explore through their therapeutic work found throughout this book. As we wade further into the experience of estrangement, I encourage you to take a deeper dive into the thoughts, feelings, and decisions of these nine women who have pondered the difficult decision to cut ties with their mothers—difficult decisions that came with plenty of fears and emotions as they navigated the *Estrangement Energy Cycle*.

Introduction to the *Estrangement Energy Cycle*

Estrangement Energy Cycle

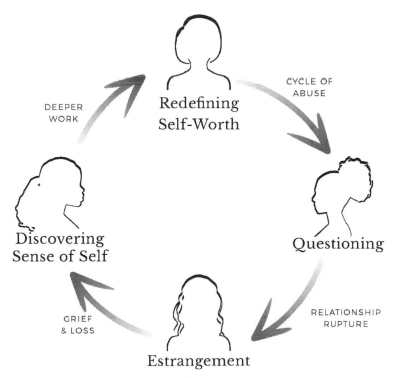

Figure 5.1. The Estrangement Energy Cycle

I F YOU ALSO WORK WITH ADULT WOMEN and trauma, it's possible that you've seen clients expend significant amounts of energy on the possibility of estrangement to protect their mental health and well-being. The decision to estrange is not impulsive, nor is it considered rash when exploring their current relationship with their mothers. For many, there is repeated discomfort, hurt, trauma, or risks to safety that push a woman to consider cutting ties with her mother. This complex, painful experience felt by dozens of female clients in therapy has led me to see a pattern in their process, a process I've come to describe as the *Estrangement Energy Cycle*.

Although a woman may seek therapy at any stage of the process, the *Estrangement Energy Cycle* starts with a pattern or **cycle of abuse**. This may be the culmination of various attachment traumas from childhood that were not acknowledged or addressed by mother, or it can be a series of events that have happened more recently in the woman's life. Either can contribute to a woman recognizing that something needs to change in order to protect her physical, emotional, and mental health within the mother-daughter relationship.

After gaining awareness about an abuse cycle, a woman can move into a stage of **questioning**. This can reflect her ambivalence about the mother-daughter relationship, including questioning her own part in it not feeling healthy or good enough. This stage can represent a woman wondering if she tries harder or communicates more effectively, maybe she can get through to mom. It could also be a questioning of an adult daughter's worthiness of love and affection from mom to a point where she tries even harder to please mom, putting her own needs on the back burner in the hopes of the relationship improving.

Therapeutically, questioning invites compassionate curiosity and exploration into the events of the mother-daughter relationship to date, including identification of possible patterns of abuse, conflict, and communication styles. This stage can serve as a safe space for clients to explore expectations of their mother-daughter relationships, where they may seek data on other mother-daughter relationships or reassurance that their relationship with mom is repairable or worth fighting for.

If a woman determines that the cycle of abuse and dynamics within the mother-daughter relationship are damaging to her health, she may then move into **relationship rupture**. This is a painful stage where the processing of the abuse and the implications for how it's shaping your client's life in the present cannot be unseen or ignored any longer. Typically an internal process where she recognizes the impact of abuse in the here and now, your adult client may have epiphanies about poor boundaries and people-pleasing, or identify a connection between her quest for perfection and seeking approval and love from mom. Relationship rupture can also be found external to the therapy room, such as an additional event of hurt or violation from mother that pushes your client from contemplation to preparation for estrangement in wanting the repeated abuse to end.

From a painful relationship rupture comes the active choice to become **estranged from mother**. This may be supported therapeutically in exploring new boundaries and preparing the client for any resistance or judgment from family and friends. The choice may weigh heavy on your client's heart and mind, resulting in a move toward grief and loss. The **grief and loss** stage includes holding space for the client's emotions and self-doubt. She may verbalize that she's not confident that she tried hard enough. Did she give up too quickly? Is the relationship reconcilable? Grief and loss includes anger at mom for what's happened as well as anger at herself if she feels that she let things go on too long or feels that she could have done more.

After extensive grief and loss work, your client will move into **discovering a new sense of self.** How will she define herself now that estrangement from mom has occurred? What will other relationships look like with healthy boundaries in place? As the result of her commitment to her own therapeutic work, she will move into a new chapter of self-realization, self-compassion, and self-confidence. Your client may seek new communities of connection and new hobbies or interests in feeling unburdened from the unhealthy relationship or repeated conflict with mom. She may also pursue activities of self-celebration, such as changing her personal appearance or making a significant or symbolic purchase to signify the changes she's experienced.

The **deeper work** comes with the support of others, whether it be a spiritual congregation, a wellness-focused community, or ongoing mental health therapy. Your client may recognize she's done all she can on her own to heal from this estrangement, but finds she needs additional support and guidance to continue the work. This may include returning to childhood injuries for deeper healing in order to move toward self-compassion and acceptance of events that have shaped her life to date.

The final stage of the *Estrangement Energy Cycle* is **redefining self-worth.** Through hard work, reflection, and developing healthy relationships with others, your client can begin to regain self-worth separate from her mother. This may be finding the bandwidth to set boundaries with others, challenging her people-pleasing urges, and practicing saying no, as just a few examples. Your client may define self-worth through self-compassion and cognitive reframes, including challenging old narratives that she discovers are mom's beliefs or mom's voice and not her own. This portion of therapy can feel especially rewarding for both you and your client, as you witness your client adopt a new, empowered way of being that feels more congruent with her values and beliefs.

Offering therapeutic support at any stage of the *Estrangement Energy Cycle* can help women begin to heal from an extremely painful situation. It's our job as trusted professionals to approach their process with abundant compassion and zero judgment. Therefore, it warrants a deeper dive into the therapeutic interventions and skills you can introduce in sessions to support your clients at each stage of the *Estrangement Energy Cycle*, starting with the cycle of abuse in the next chapter.

Cycle of Abuse

6

AS WE MOVE FURTHER INTO the estrangement experience along-side our clients within therapy, it is important to recognize the circumstances that can lead to an eventual mother–daughter relationship rupture. By no means is this an exhaustive list; however, here are some negative relational patterns and traumas to explore clinically:

- power and control,
- gaslighting,
- financial abuse,
- generational trauma,
- minimizing,
- scapegoating,
- caregiving,
- defective/denial, and
- superior parenting.

Power and Control

A relationship where a mother desires power and control over her daughter is a tumultuous one, to say the least. The daughter may respond by acting out and seeking autonomy for herself, sometimes at a young age, or she may try to compensate for mom's lack of caring and acceptance by enabling mom's behavior in the hopes of eventually winning her affection. Either way, a daughter may question whether she made the right choice with mom, much like Regina did as a young adult.

Regina watched her mom align with her stepfather, who disciplined Regina as a young girl whenever she failed to do what he asked. Unfortunately, this was not the end of Regina's abuse. She was also subjected to sexual abuse by her sibling and his friends. Instead of mom siding with Regina and protecting her as Regina desperately wanted her to, Regina recalls her mother ignoring her pleas for help when her stepfather was punishing her, aligning with him to maintain the greatest power and control within the household.

Gaslighting

The phenomenon of gaslighting was memorably portrayed in the 1944 film *Gaslight* directed by George Cukor. Gaslighting describes manipulation of the other person by denying their experiences and perceptions to the point of them questioning their own sanity. Gaslighting can sound like "you're wrong," "I didn't say that," or "you're acting crazy." In essence, it's any communication that puts the blame or focus on the other person so the gaslighter can continue their negative behavior without consequence. When gaslighting is defined and explored in depth, women who've been subjected to it within their relationships can feel shocked, angry, embarrassed, and outraged.

Summer felt gaslighted by her mom for her choice of wanting to live with her grandma, who she felt was a better parent than her mom, Cher. Cher liked to party and didn't hold down a steady job for several years. When Summer's grandma got sick, Summer welcomed the opportunity to live with her full time. Summer discovered her caregiving side from a young age, but was devastated when her grandma died from her illnesses a year later. Instead of returning to mom's house, she decided to live with friends while finishing high school, to which her mom responded with escalating gaslighting, ridicule, and disdain. The more Summer's mom gaslit her choices of responsibility, independence, and wanting to finish high school and go to college, the more Summer felt pushed to build a life free from what she called Cher's antics, including the partying lifestyle.

Financial Abuse

Abuse can take many forms, including financial. Financial abuse can take the guise of wanting to help someone get out of debt or get back on their feet, but it comes at a cost. The person holding the finances has all the control, meaning they can withhold funds, intercept paychecks, and require the person to justify purchases or seek permission to spend.

Kasey was surprised to learn that financial abuse was an experience that described her relationship with her mom, Cindy. When Kasey found herself struggling with alcohol in college, Cindy stepped in to control her finances, locking down her accounts and confiscating her credit cards. After several false starts and relapses, Kasey was eager to regain mom's trust in celebrating three months of sobriety. Instead of working with Kasey to return financial responsibility back to her as an adult, Cindy began demanding more and more of Kasey, including expecting her to earn her money privileges back and pay rent, even though Kasey hadn't yet secured a job.

Generational Trauma

Mark Wolynn's (2017) book, *It Didn't Start With You*, had a powerful ripple effect on various communities because it offered insight into generational trauma and repeated adversity. The concept of trauma altering genetic material and being passed down from generation to generation was eye-opening and affirming to populations large and small.

Kathryn had read about generational trauma as part of her own personal growth. She believed the cycle of abuse from her grandmother to her mother to her contributed to her fighting personality and nononsense attitude as an adult. Kathryn was outraged that her mother perpetuated the same cycle of abuse by allowing her grandfather to berate and demean Kathryn when she was young. Kathryn's mother acknowledged her own abuse as a child but denied that Kathryn was being abused by her grandfather, prompting Kathryn to move out on her own at the age of fourteen. In therapy, Kathryn found herself reflecting on the similarities between her mother's behaviors and Kathryn's choice in men as dating partners with a similar personality. She recognized it was a subconscious choice of the devil you know versus the devil you don't.

Minimizing

Discounting one's experiences and conveying a message that the person is overreacting is defined as minimizing. This can be especially damaging when applied to a person's trauma experience. When the person whose experience is being minimized realizes that they've been subjected to trauma at the hands of a loved one, it can propel them toward a relationship rupture.

Keisha felt minimized by her mother. Her mom, Jeanie, would threaten her and banish her from the house during Jeanie's boyfriend's visits, and then tell Keisha she was overreacting when Keisha would express her hurt and anger at how she was treated. Arriving home early one night resulted in Keisha being pushed against a wall with her arms pinned by Jeanie, who proceeded to threaten her, which catapulted Keisha into pursuing estrangement soon after.

Scapegoating

First brought to my attention by Claudia Black's (1990) book, *Double Duty: Dual Dynamics Within the Chemically Dependent Home*, scapegoating describes the blaming of all bad things on another person (or thing), regardless of whether they are at fault. The wrongdoings can be blatantly not theirs to own, and after a series of scapegoating events, the targeted person may feel fed up or desire space away from the person to be free from undeserved blame.

Nina was the scapegoat in her family for years. She recalled, as a young child, being blamed for her mother's back pain and headaches because of her appearance. When she didn't meet her mother's expectations of how to look and act, her mother labeled her as a problem child, even going so far as to claim that Nina suffered from bipolar disorder to anyone who would listen. Nina felt attacked and misunderstood, but didn't feel like she could fight back because she had received consistent messaging in childhood that moms know best and should be respected. Instead, she swallowed her emotions with food, binge eating to feel disgusting on the inside to match how her mom made her feel about her looks on the outside.

Caregiving

In contrast to youth and adults who rebel against inaccurate and hurtful labels, there are others who attempt to earn their parent's love and approval with their actions, including caregiving from a young age. These children tend to grow up fast, recognizing that they are celebrated by their parents for taking care of themselves and others.

Toni defined her value and worth in her ability to be a quality caregiver to others. When she found herself frustrated that her efforts with mom, Jan, were not more effective in stopping Jan's cycling depression, Toni turned to nurturing others in her community and within the workplace to feel worthwhile. Toni especially loved taking care of babies and pets, feeling warmth and love from them in return for her efforts. She was surprised to discover that her career choice within the medical field also fed into this deeper wound of wanting to be good enough and loved by others.

Defective/Denial

The concept of being good enough is foundational for many women who have experienced trauma, especially attachment trauma with their mothers. As a result, they may harbor negative core beliefs of being unworthy, unlovable, or defective. Core beliefs create a visceral reaction in people, especially when voiced out loud to others. I've introduced the exercise of discovering core beliefs through a tree analogy, working our way into the roots of the tree. I've also warned clients that they would know they were close to identifying their core belief when thinking about it or voicing it would result in tears, choked speech, or nausea. After all, we elect to keep negative core beliefs buried and hidden most of the time because of how painful they can be.

Enid looked put together from the outside. She had a decent job, a loving boyfriend, and roommates who enjoyed doing things together on weekends. It was only in therapy that she felt she could voice her deepest concerns of being defective and gross. Enid had been sexually molested by a family member when she was a child. She refused to recognize the molestation's impact on her personal identity as an adult, at least until it would rear its ugly head at the most inconvenient times. Enid suffered from panic attacks and sexual intimacy blocks, reporting she would feel gross or disgusting when being sexual with her partner. She could no longer deny the impact of the abuse on her sense of self, coming to therapy with a goal of stopping the negative thoughts and feelings.

Superior Parenting

A common fear for women who have been wronged by their moms is finding themselves helpless to prevent becoming just like them. It can lead to vehement disclosures that they will do everything in their power to be better moms to their own children, stopping the painful cycle that shaped their childhood. This can lead to workaholism and perfectionism for women driven to have things look and feel different. They may show up to therapy feeling burnt out, fatigued, and frustrated with the lack of momentum in their plans to have a different life, and can struggle with boundaries, such as saying no to requests from others at home and in the workplace.

Knowingly compensating for the trauma of what came before, Charlotte was vocal about wanting to be a very different parent from her mother. She adopted a fierceness over her children's safety, stemming from her own childhood abuse and neglect. In order to reassure herself that she was not, in fact, becoming her mother, Charlotte went above and beyond to schedule educational experiences for her children, becoming a super mom who balanced responsibilities around the house with activities catered to creating a quality childhood for each of them. Unfortunately, this led to a decline in her own mental health and self-care in putting her children's needs before her own.

As these examples illustrate, we will continue to focus on trauma and abuse as catalysts for estrangement throughout this book. As a mental health therapist, I know healing can happen in a variety of ways, with some cases showing reconciliation as a possibility. Regardless of an eventual outcome of estrangement or reconciliation, it's important to emphasize that the choice is completely the client's. Their identification with a cycle of abuse can be a primary motivator for engaging in the therapeutic space with a neutral party, especially if they've experienced unsolicited opinions and unhelpful judgments when vocalizing their hurt to others.

Questioning

7

ONCE A CYCLE OF ABUSE IS IDENTIFIED, the client may elect to continue therapy when entering a stage of questioning. This stage offers a multitude of questions and concerns to explore therapeutically, including the immediate and long-lasting effects of the abuse and possible outcomes they can pursue to regain control and autonomy over their life. Questioning includes a client's exploration into their own actions and choices in the face of abuse, with the holding of space by their therapist being paramount to the client engaging in cognitive reframes and self-compassion work to start the healing process.

Shame and Guilt

Kasey was quick to identify shame and guilt within her questioning stage. Her mom, Cindy, had reinforced messages over the years of Kasey being untrustworthy due to alcohol abuse and claiming that Kasey was overly emotional. Kasey felt responsible for not being there for her mom in Cindy's own alcohol abuse and sudden death, motivating Kasey to continue therapy. The biggest element of questioning for Kasey was exploring the messages her six-year-old self received about expressing emotions. Through gentle challenging, she determined that the expectations placed on six-year-old Kasey to be composed and stoic through several traumatic experiences was unreasonable and hurtful, resulting in her suppressing her darker emotions in alcohol to transform into the happy, gregarious version of herself that others had come to expect.

Negative Core Beliefs

Working to identify her negative core beliefs (see Exercise 7.1), Toni discovered fears of being unworthy and unlovable. She recognized this was in part due to her experience with her mom's repetitive depressive episodes. Toni uncovered deep sadness that she was not worth Jan getting out of bed to care for her when she was younger, and recognized that she was trying to compensate and convince herself (and mom) that she was worth the effort.

EXERCISE 7.1.   **Negative Core Beliefs Tree**

Step 1: Grab a piece of paper or download our handout at estrange mentenergycycle.com. Self-worth is deeply rooted in beliefs we carry based on the earliest experiences we have in life. To make these beliefs more approachable to self-discovery, let's use a tree visual. Draw a picture of a tree with leaves, trunk, and roots or download our handout for a tree template.

Step 2: The worries and anxieties we are consciously aware of are the leaves of the tree. These are the things we can easily verbalize such as stressors and concerns. Things like "I'm always late. I feel like a bad friend. I'm always running late. I don't stand up for myself." What are your worries and anxieties related to your relationship with your mom? Write them in the leaves of the tree.

Step 3: Going deeper cognitively, we ask ourselves what these thoughts say about us, which gets us to the trunk of our tree. We may recognize thoughts like, "I'm lazy. I'm a slacker. I'm a bad friend." Write down key phrases or thoughts on the trunk of your tree.

Step 4: We continue to ask ourselves the question, "if this is true about me, what does this say about me?" to go even deeper, in order to get to the roots of the tree. The roots represent the negative core beliefs that drive our behaviors and can feel painful to explore—negative core beliefs like "I am unlovable. I'm a failure. I'm unworthy." Capture your negative core beliefs in the roots of your tree.

Step 5: Now that you are aware of your negative core beliefs, what would you prefer to believe? Write the opposite of your negative core beliefs or another, more positive belief to the side of your tree. Make sure it's an "I" statement! Try on statements like "I am lovable as I am. I'm trying the best I can. I am worthy." Which are easier to embrace or accept?

Self-Doubt

Nina had been subjected to her mother's emotional abuse since she was little. Although she could access her logical side in knowing the hurtful things her mother said weren't true, her series of failed, unhealthy relationships made her question if what her mom said about her had more merit than she initially wanted to admit. She worried that she'd heard the labels and hurtful attacks on her looks and character enough times that they felt like truths in her emotional mind. Nina was tasked in therapy to slow down the self-doubt spiral and access the dialectical behavioral therapy (DBT) concept of Wise Mind (see Exercise 7.2) in order to identify her thoughts and feelings as separate from her mom's.

EXERCISE 7.2.   **Dialectical Behavioral Therapy (DBT) Wise Mind**

Step 1: Draw a Venn Diagram or download our handout at estrange mentenergycycle.com. Label the left circle "logic" and the right circle "emotion."

Step 2: When thinking about your relationship with your mother, what emotions show up? List them in the **emotion** circle (e.g., sadness, anger, outrage, shock, denial, grief).

Step 3: When thinking about your relationship with your mother, what dynamics or facts can you name that are grounded in **logic**? List them in the logic circle (e.g., my mom is depressed, my mom has her own trauma, she's lashing out, I am the child of an emotionally immature parent, this mistreatment is a form of abuse, I want this pattern to stop, we can repair, this can get better).

Step 4: **Wise Mind** is the intersection of emotion and logic. When you hold space in your mind for both your emotions and logic, what do you hear or see? What needs to happen to support your autonomy in the mother-daughter relationship? What are your next steps to remain grounded and in control of your own actions? Write these in the intersection of your Venn Diagram that is Wise Mind.

Emotion Dysregulation

Kathryn continued to struggle with regulating her emotions on an almost daily basis. She reported she was lashing out at her child as well as complete strangers, which was impacting her ability to perform tasks at work and at home. Kathryn's therapeutic task in the questioning stage included cultivating curiosity about the messages behind her anger, in order to better understand it. As with an onion, she had to bravely peel back the layers with tears in her eyes, to uncover what was hidden behind the rage.

The Burden of Busyness

Summer had learned about attachment styles in therapy to better understand her avoidant attachment response in adulthood. She had embraced independence at a young age to prevent her return to a home that felt unstable due to the chosen lifestyle and gaslighting behavior of her mom, Cher. What Summer didn't realize about growing up so fast was that it would influence her to take on more and more responsibilities in a frenzied sense of busyness. She found herself in a constant state of anxiety trying to juggle things as a young mom and graduate student, yet openly admitted to staying busy and choosing anxiety over other negative feelings that would inevitably show up in idle moments. The therapy office became her safe place to slow down and give herself permission to feel the feelings she was avoiding under the burden of busyness.

Active Avoidance

Similar to Summer, Enid was aware of her avoidant behaviors in response to traumas in her past and present. She prided herself on not letting them define her—that is, until they manifested as anxiety and dissociation at inopportune times. As her therapist, I challenged her to question the connection between her somatic complaints of panic attacks, numbness, and hypervigilance with the trauma she was actively ignoring and avoiding.

Self-Criticism

When Keisha would get phone calls after violent encounters with her mom, Jeanie—who acted like nothing happened—instead of being angry with her, Keisha would turn to questioning herself. Were her expectations of an apology from mom too high? Was she preventing a quality relationship between her kids and their grandma? Was she over-reacting? Keisha pursued the therapeutic space to explore her options of reconciling with her mom with some new boundaries in place or continuing to keep her at arm's length.

Suicidal Ideation

Not all estrangement feels like it can be resolved or reconciled easily. Sexual and physical abuse had impacted Regina significantly, stunting her emotional intelligence and functioning to the physical age of her assaults. Regina also pinpointed her suicidal thoughts appearing at the same time, creating chronic suicidality that brought her comfort in knowing if things didn't improve, she could die by suicide. As you can imagine, this scenario scares many clinicians, especially as Regina would frequently vocalize that she was unsure she wanted to live with the abuse that haunted her. Fortunately, Regina was both blunt and honest about her suicidal thoughts in therapy, readily scaling them in her process of questioning how to heal from abuse from multiple perpetrators within her family.

Perfectionism

One element that is common for women exploring estrangement from their mothers is perfectionism. Charlotte was no exception in her mantra of "I can do better." Her perfectionism manifested as wanting to be the perfect mom, wishing to attend to her children's needs flawlessly and with rock-steady composure. Therapy was a place for her to reclaim her humanness by questioning her desires for perfection and learning that she could make mistakes and still be a worthwhile human being and loving mom to her kids.

As the above experiences of our nine clients illustrate, the questioning phase of the *Estrangement Energy Cycle* encapsulates both internal and external exploration with a big helping of compassionate curiosity from their therapeutic provider. This stage can serve to help clients move from contemplation to preparation, by identifying their overall desire for change. Questioning can uncover a lot of hurt and uncertainty, which may leave clients not feeling fully prepared for how it accelerates them into possible relationship rupture, which is our next stage to explore.

Relationship Rupture

As the client better understands the cycle of abuse and explores its implications through questioning, a heaviness can set in. This heaviness represents the elements she is still processing, such as, "why did this happen to me? Why couldn't it have been different? Why wasn't my mom like other moms?" The client has since identified elements within the mother-daughter relationship that are deeply dissatisfying, traumatic, or hurtful, recognizing things that she can no longer suppress or ignore. This new awareness can prompt the client to attempt to set new boundaries with mom.

Charlotte's boundary was to separate from mom both physically and emotionally by moving away. She recognized that she didn't trust her mom, Sandra, to be around her children and keep them safe, and felt pressure from her spouse to relocate closer to his side of the family for additional childcare support.

Kathryn, too, moved out of reach of her mom at the younger age of fourteen. She was angry at mom's passivity in how Kathryn's grandfather treated her and felt she needed to create space from both of them to feel healthy.

As clinicians, we know how important emotional and physical boundaries can be. In fact, Coleman (2021) believes that therapists are at risk of encouraging estrangement because of our championing of boundaries with our clients. Although boundaries are a common therapeutic goal, I disagree that there's a causal relationship between supporting our clients with developing boundaries and pushing estrangement as the best option, especially because of how emotionally painful the estrangement process can be. But back to boundaries. There's a reason for the saying "those who push back against your boundaries the most are the ones who benefited from you having none."

When working on boundaries with clients, I always share how it's easier to practice new, healthy boundaries with strangers or coworkers first, leaving the more difficult family boundaries for last. This is partly due to how long the family system has experienced the unhealthy boundaries and the natural resistance to the new boundaries that arises in family members—a resistance that shows up to maintain a level of homeostasis or dysfunction the family has come to expect. In the relationship rupture stage, if new boundaries are attempted and mother violates them, the client may feel more frustrated or angry than previous attempts. This is due in part to the client's deeper awareness of unhealthy relationship patterns, and their motivation to disrupt the pattern in their mother-daughter relationship. A client may feel like they are at a new emotional limit in wanting the painful pattern to end, resulting in a more serious look at relationship rupture as an option.

After several attempts to broach the subject of mom Jeanie's violent behavior regarding boyfriends, Keisha found herself fed up. She recognized that her inner critic attacked her every time she gave Jeanie a chance to do better, but then found herself hurt again by Jeanie's actions or words instead.

Toni was tired of feeling helpless in the face of mom Jan's depression. She knew that expecting mom to overcome depression after so many years of drowning in symptoms wasn't realistic or helpful. She wanted to redefine expectations of interactions with her mom and knew she needed to let old hopes and goals go in order to do so.

In addition to an internal shift in boundaries for women at this stage, relationship rupture can occur if there is another incident that threatens to further damage or harm the client or her hopes for the mother-daughter relationship.

Kasey found herself packing a bag and keeping it by her front door in response to escalating fights and attempts to control her by her mother. Cindy had threatened to evict Kasey from the family condo she was staying in, and having her own set of keys, showed up multiple times uninvited to see if Kasey was sober. Rather than engage in another conflict, Kasey began screening her calls and felt on edge most nights, recognizing it was only a matter of time before mom showed up at the door and demanded she leave.

To feel more in control of her surroundings, Summer had moved several states away from her childhood home. When she planned to visit other family members in her home state on holidays, she was adamant that they not post any pictures or evidence of her visits on social media. Summer shared she made this request in feeling overcome with anxiety at the possibility that mom Cher would show up at a family function where Summer would feel trapped into engaging her. Avoidant and panicked by this idea, Summer did everything in her power to avoid the possibility of an encounter.

Nina was not as successful in her attempts to avoid her mom. Things had escalated to a point where other family members were disinviting Nina to family events because of the things Nina's mom said about her. One day, Nina's mom showed up at a family event Nina was still welcome to attend, and proceeded to verbally attack her, conveniently away from the curious stares of other family members. This resulted in a physical altercation where Nina was charged with physical assault against her mom. Nina was arrested and ejected from future family functions, finding herself further ostracized and alone.

Navigating the ripple effect of a mother-daughter relationship rupture on other family members requires additional energy for adult women exploring possible estrangement. They may feel judged or criticized for not fighting hard enough to preserve the relationship, or be accused of giving up too easily in the eyes of their family. Feeling the loss of mom is painful enough, yet many women feel the loss of additional members of their family who side with mom or turn their backs on your client, believing their actions to be petty, dramatic, or impulsive. This can result in the client feeling even more alone and hurt as they come to terms with the reality that they've lost multiple relationships in their attempts to set healthy boundaries.

Enid felt outraged that her grandma was asking her to choose between her mom and herself. Her grandma's opinion was that Enid's mom's addiction was ruling her life and causing her to spiral out of control, resulting in grandma writing her off years ago. Grandma believed Enid should do the same, adding pressure to Enid as she explored how to have a relationship with mom at the risk of losing a relationship with her grandma if she succeeded.

Regina recognized that she had to be careful who to engage within her extended family, finding herself testing their allegiance before opening herself up to trusting them. She explained in therapy how she'd ask each member what they knew about her abuse and how they felt about it. If a family member was nonchalant or appeared in alignment with mom and stepdad in any way, Regina would disengage and block them from contacting her again. If they expressed sadness and surprise at what she'd been through, she found herself more willing to cultivate a relationship with them. Regina's black-and-white thinking about who to let into her life came from a childhood desire for control and autonomy, in an otherwise chaotic and abusive household. It made sense that she was trying to screen her relationships in adulthood in ways where she maintained the power of choice, especially when she didn't have that power as a child.

The relationship rupture stage presents a meaningful shift for women exploring their mother-daughter relationship needs. They could choose to continue to evaluate the relationship in pursuit of change, or accept it for what it is. However, women working through this process in a therapeutic setting find themselves more ready and willing to consider estrangement in uncovering the damaging, traumatic experiences that shaped their childhood or adulthood. The increased possibility of estrangement can be motivated by their pursuit of the healthy boundaries they deserve in their relationships. It could also be that they've explored their fears and the worst-case outcomes of estrangement thoroughly, choosing to courageously move forward with estrangement in pursuit of their own mental health and wellness.

Therapeutic Tools for Estrangement Energy

WE CAN AGREE THAT ESTRANGEMENT is an extremely difficult and complex decision that is chosen for various reasons. Once an adult daughter moves forward with the decision to pursue estrangement from her mother, it can take several intentional steps for estrangement to feel real, ranging on a spectrum of actively notifying mom that they don't want to have contact, to disengaging and distancing over time in a more passive approach.

Regardless of the means of getting there, women will feel a barrage of emotions in coming to terms with their estrangement status. Therapeutically, it's our job as mental health professionals to maintain compassionate curiosity of the cognitions and emotions that show up for our clients at this stage, especially since estrangement energy can feel strange, stigmatizing, and full of grief. It's often an experience where clients don't yet feel that they have their footing.

Therefore, it's important to anticipate and normalize the variety of thoughts, feelings, behaviors, and reactions that embody estrangement energy. Our adult female clients may experience the following, or may bring with them into the therapy room for further processing. Estrangement energy elements include

- shutting down the inner critic,
- experiencing anticipatory grief,
- challenging ambivalence,
- exploring forgiveness,
- understanding the fight-or-flight response,
- addressing elevated anxiety,

- watching for warning signs,
- exploring EMDR, and
- staying present.

Shutting Down the Inner Critic

For Nina, part of her estrangement status was recognizing how the physical violence that took place with her mom served as an indicator of how unhealthy her relationship with her mother had become. Even though she could acknowledge the separation as a logical next step, she continued to subject herself to self-criticism and the criticism of other members of the family. A turning point for Nina was learning to personify her inner critic in order to separate herself from it to achieve emotion regulation (see Exercise 9.1). Once she was able to step back from criticism and experience it separate from herself, she regained confidence in her ability to control her emotions and told her inner critic to take a seat. Nina's epiphany in therapy came from discovering that her inner critic's voice was her mother's and so began the task of finding her own voice to successfully take back emotional control.

EXERCISE 9.1.   **Inner Critic Personification**

Step 1: Have a piece of paper and pen nearby or download our handout at estrangementenergycycle.com. Get into a comfortable position and close your eyes or put them at rest (e.g., looking down and softening your gaze). When you bring your attention inward and allow yourself to feel your inner critic, what does it look like? What represents it best, a person or an object? How do you feel toward it? Write down what you are noticing.

Step 2: Now that you know your inner critic, can you talk to it as if it's a separate entity to help reduce its power? Notice when it likes to show up. What it says to you. What do you want to say to it now that you are feeling more separate from it? Write down some things you can say.

Step 3: Picture a container in your mind to hold your inner critic now that you know it better. Visualize placing it in the container, focusing on the container size, material, and shape. Once your inner critic is successfully inside the container, visualize sealing it and placing it somewhere safe to allow your mind, body, and emotions to regulate. Note your container size, shape, and location on your piece of paper for future reference.

Experiencing Anticipatory Grief

Watching her relationship with her mom spiral out of control before her eyes, Kasey knew that things were headed in the wrong direction. Her mother's verbal attacks and threats to evict her from the one thing that felt stable in her life led Kasey to enter anticipatory grief. Anticipatory grief, for many clients, is a grief response showing up before the loss occurs—sometimes weeks, months, or years before the loss is experienced! In the case of Kasey, she could see the writing on the wall that without mom Cindy's willingness to have a rational conversation with her (or possible family therapy to address all of the hurtful accusations), Kasey was going to have to break contact with her to protect her mental health and sobriety. Anticipatory grief led to Kasey discovering her love of writing, as she began to write "divorce letters," first to her addiction and then to her mom, Cindy (see Exercise 9.2). This allowed her to speak her truth and say the things her mom wouldn't let her say in real time in response to conflict. Kasey was able to process healthy grief and loss through her letters, which, unbeknownst to Kasey, prepared her for Cindy's sudden death several months later.

EXERCISE 9.2.   **Letter of Divorce**

Step 1: Grab a piece of paper or download our handout at estrange mentenergycycle.com. A letter of divorce signifies a separation in a relationship that originates in substance abuse and recovery work, specifically divorcing your addiction. Rather than being exclusively used for this purpose, consider what you would write to your mom related to the stressors or strain in your relationship. Jot some things down.

Step 2: Allow yourself to write freely and with full emotion. Avoid self-censoring as this writing is for your eyes only. What are you noticing? What themes are coming up that are worthwhile to note or to continue to work on at a deeper level? Note the themes on your piece of paper.

Step 3: Read your divorce letter out loud, recognizing how it makes you feel to hear in your own voice.

Step 4: To honor the difficult and vulnerable work you've just done, what is the next appropriate step? Do you want to hold onto this letter as part of your work? Would you benefit from releasing yourself from it, such as tearing it up or burning it? Do what makes you feel most comfortable. Remember, you can write as many drafts or letters as you need to, to fully express yourself.

Challenging Ambivalence

Do I give her another chance? This was Keisha's ongoing question for herself that she brought into the therapy room. She admitted she was really struggling with her children not having a relationship with their grandma, and found herself wondering if she could tolerate mom Jeanie's behavior toward her so Jeanie could be an involved grandparent to the kids. Keisha benefited from the cognitive behavioral therapy (CBT) exercise of best–worst–most likely scenarios (see Exercise 9.3) to explore this further. By carving out space in the therapy office to think through the best-case scenario, worst-case scenario, and most likely scenario, Keisha felt that she could make an intentional, informed choice for herself and her children regarding contact with Jeanie.

EXERCISE 9.3.   **Cognitive Behavioral Therapy (CBT) Best–Worst–Most Likely**

Step 1: Grab a piece of paper or download our handout at estrange mentenergycycle.com. When thinking about your relationship with your mother, identify a scenario you've been contemplating such as confronting, allowing a relationship with your children, reconnecting, disconnecting, or inviting her to the holidays.

Step 2: What comes to mind as the best-case outcome in your scenario? Write it down.

Step 3: What comes to mind as the worst-case outcome in your scenario? Write it down.

Step 4: What comes to mind as the most likely outcome in your scenario? Write it down.

Step 5: Reread your responses to best, worst, and most likely scenarios and sit with any emotions that come up. How does this influence your decision? Based on what you've discovered, where do you go from here?

Exploring Forgiveness

Regina had heard from many well-meaning family members and strangers that she should forgive her mother for not being there for her through her childhood abuse. Regina found herself further pressured into forgiveness by the church she joined with her spouse. Although she recognized a part of her desperately wanted to find forgiveness in missing a relationship with her mother, Regina recognized it was much more complicated than reaching out and reconnecting. In therapy, Regina embarked on the emotionally charged and enlightening journey of mapping out her trauma family tree (see Exercise 9.4). Through the visual of seeing how trauma connected her not just to her mom, but to her dad, stepdad, and brother, Regina realized she could not safely engage mom without the risk of being reconnected to her stepdad and brother, both of whom she preferred to remain estranged from as they were the primary perpetrators of her abuse. Regina found that the therapeutic exercise helped her solidify her decision to remain estranged, and helped her spouse further understand her decision when she shared it with him.

EXERCISE 9.4. **Trauma Family Tree**

Step 1: Grab a piece of paper or download our handout at estrange mentenergycycle.com. Start by mapping out your family tree, with you in the middle and noting partner/spouse, children, parents, grandparents, and extended family if appropriate and desired.

Step 2: Indicate the level of connection between you and each family member. A solid line indicates a connection. A double solid line indicates closeness in the relationship. A dashed line indicates a relationship that is now distant such as divorce, separation, or estrangement. A broken line indicates no relationship of any kind.

Step 3: Write down key facts that you are aware of about each person next to their name. Note things like age, occupation, mental health history, substance use history, abuse history, and fighting style.

Step 4: What trends do you see, if any, related to the key factors listed above? Is there a theme of helping professionals in the family? A string of divorces? A common fighting style of yelling or avoiding? Mental health of anxiety and depression present from generation to generation? Abuse cycles from grandparent to parent to child? Estrangement in multiple relationships or generations within the family tree?

Step 5: Further notice what emotions and sensations arise for you as you look at your family tree. What emotions do you feel? What clarity can this exercise bring you at this stage in your life? What cycles or patterns do you wish to break in your generation or your children's generation?

Understanding the Fight-or-Flight Response

Enid was tasked with communicating openly with her new boyfriend about her complicated family dynamic, including the pressure to estrange from her mother. A self-proclaimed expert at avoiding, she couldn't hide her feelings from him any longer when he witnessed an argument between her and her grandma, followed by her having a panic attack. Instead of ignoring her feelings, Enid was challenged to better understand her response to conflict and her desire to run away from the problem. When she found herself on the edge of a panic attack or a fight-or-flight response, she agreed to practice the 5-4-3-2-1 mindfulness technique (see Exercise 9.5), to bring her back into her body in the present moment. By practicing this technique in the therapy room first, she built up confidence in her ability to regulate around her family, who she felt knew all too well how to push her buttons.

EXERCISE 9.5.   **5-4-3-2-1**

*(Grab the script and an audio file
for download at estrangementenergycycle.com.)*

Step 1: Take note of your surroundings and begin with three belly breaths.

Step 2: What are 5 things that are blue (or any color you pick)? Name them in your mind or out loud.

Step 3: What are 4 things you can hear? Name them in your mind or out loud.

Step 4: What are 3 things you can touch? Name them in your mind or out loud.

Step 5: What are 2 things you can smell? Name them in your mind or out loud.

Step 6: What is 1 thing you can taste? Name it in your mind or out loud.

The five senses can be in any order. Notice how your mind calms in having a task that prevents rumination on other, more stressful topics. Repeat this exercise as many times as needed!

Addressing Elevated Anxiety

Recalling her anxiety having appeared after her grandma died, Summer didn't know what it was like to live without it. She had embraced a life of barely controlled chaos to feed the anxiety and channel it into busyness and productivity. Having been estranged from her mom, Cher, for years prior to coming to therapy, she knew she experienced elevated anxiety when planning trips to her hometown out of fear of running into Cher. In therapy, Summer identified additional layers of anxiety tied to mother-inspired holidays, trauma anniversaries, and milestones with her own young daughter. To keep her anxiety in check, she learned the thought-stopping technique (see Exercise 9.6). This allowed Summer to stay present for her daughter in managing her anxiety and allowed her the energy and motivation to pursue healthy relationships with chosen family members instead.

EXERCISE 9.6.   **Thought-Stopping Technique**
*(Grab the script and an audio file for download
at estrangementenergycycle.com.)*

Step 1: Identify a negative thought that you are having in this moment.
Step 2: Ask yourself, what is the evidence of the thought being true?
Step 3: Ask yourself, what is the evidence of the thought being false?
Step 4: Ask yourself, is this a fact or feeling?
Step 5: Ask yourself, why am I having this feeling? What was the trigger?
Step 6: Ask yourself, what am I going to do now with these feelings?

Watching for Warning Signs

Depression can be extremely difficult on family members, and Toni was no exception. Her strategy was to grow apart from her mom, Jan, as soon as Jan was able to move out of Toni's living room, where she'd been staying since her last depressive episode months before. Feeling restless and depleted, Toni struggled to remember what she liked to do for fun when she wasn't trying to win Jan's love. Toni was given homework between therapy sessions to complete with her spouse, which included identifying warning signs for when she was backsliding into caregiving and people-pleasing, followed by finding activities—both active and quiet, solo and together (see Exercise 9.7)—that she could schedule as part of her self-care in her estrangement process.

EXERCISE 9.7.   **Watch Your Warning Signs**

Step 1: Grab a piece of paper or download our handout at estrange mentenergycycle.com. Draw four quadrants. For the top two boxes, write "Physical" in one box and "Psychological" in the other. For the left side of the quadrants, label one "Wellness" and one "Decline."

Step 2: Write the physical symptoms you recognize in yourself for Physical Wellness in the appropriate box. Write the physical symptoms you recognize in yourself for Physical Decline in the appropriate box.

Step 3: Write the psychological symptoms you recognize in yourself for Psychological Wellness in the appropriate box. Write the psychological symptoms you recognize in yourself for Psychological Decline in the appropriate box. Note if any of the decline warning signs are present for you in this time of your life.

Step 4: Next, draw a second 4-box quadrant for self-care or download our handout at estrangementenergycycle.com. For the top two boxes, write "Quiet" and "Active." For the left side of the quadrants, label one "Together" and the other "Alone."

Step 5: Write self-care ideas that are quiet and together in the appropriate box. Write self-care strategies that are active and together in the appropriate box.

Step 6: Write self-care strategies for quiet and alone in the appropriate box. Write self-care ideas that are active and alone in the appropriate box.

Step 7: Check your calendar. Where can you schedule self-care each week? Which of these self-care options can you implement right away versus planning ahead for them in your calendar?

Exploring EMDR

Will I pass this trauma to my daughter? That was Kathryn's question in her therapeutic work after uncovering the hurt and pain of her mother-daughter relationship beneath the angry exterior. She had made herself sick with worry that her daughter would inherit the trauma of the women who came before her, especially if Kathryn couldn't get her rage under control. Kathryn was interested in eye movement desensitization and reprocessing (EMDR) to address the abuse of her childhood that involved her grandfather and mother. She spent several sessions engaging in EMDR resourcing to avoid flooding her already volatile system, crafting her EMDR resourcing toolkit (see Exercise 9.8), to support herself both in therapy and when interacting with others. These tools came in handy as Kathryn attempted to reduce arguments with her daughter. The resourcing also assisted Kathryn in evaluating the status of estrangement with her mother from a newfound calm, level-headed place.

EXERCISE 9.8.   **Eye Movement Desensitization and Reprocessing (EMDR) Resource List**

Step 1: Grab a piece of paper or download our handout at estrange mentenergycycle.com. On your paper, draw a table that is two boxes wide and three boxes long for a total of six boxes. Label each of the boxes: (1) Supports/People (2) Things/Habits/Behaviors (3) Beliefs/Thoughts (4) Self-Soothing (5) Safe/Helpful/Positive Places (6) Active/Passive Coping

Step 2: Fill out examples in each box that are applicable to you. If you get stuck, ask a loved one or someone who knows you really well what they see that calms you under stress. This can add insight and ideas to your worksheet. The goal is to have multiple possibilities for positive coping in each box when responding to trauma or stress symptoms.

Step 3: Gather any tangible items you've identified in your resource list to keep at the ready. For example, perhaps you have a fidget tool on your keyring, have built a playlist of songs that elevate your mood, or keep mints or essential oils in your bag to help ground you.

Staying Present

Charlotte was shocked to hear from her mother after decades of separation. She brought her confusion, hope, and trepidation into her therapy sessions in the hopes of figuring out how to respond to her mother's outreach and request to talk. In the voicemail Charlotte received, her mother, Sandra, offered an apology for all that happened in Charlotte's childhood, stating she was at fault and that she'd been working on herself over the last several years. She invited Charlotte to call her back so she could share how things had changed, in the hopes that Sandra could have a relationship with her grandchildren. Charlotte recognized her knee-jerk reaction to distance and dissociate, much as she had to do as a child experiencing repeated sexual abuse. She decided to revisit her five senses coping kit from previous therapy sessions (see Exercise 9.9), to focus on staying calm and present when engaging Sandra to explore a possible reconciliation. Charlotte knew she needed to feel clear headed and grounded in order to set realistic expectations for any planned interaction with her mom.

EXERCISE 9.9.   **Five Senses Coping Kit**

Step 1: Grab a piece of paper or download our handout at estrange mentenergycycle.com. Write down the five senses across your paper as See, Smell, Taste, Touch, and Hear.

Step 2: Reflect on what images calm you when you are upset or stressed. Write down ideas under the "See" column.

Step 3: Reflect on what smells bring you comfort. Write down ideas under the "Smell" column.

Step 4: Reflect on what tastes are nostalgic or comforting to you. Write them down under the "Taste" column.

Step 5: Reflect on what things you like to touch that bring you comfort. Are they smooth? Soft? Warm or cold? Write down ideas under the "Touch" column.

Step 6: Reflect on things you can hear that are comforting—things like nature sounds or music. Write down ideas under the "Hear" column.

Step 7: Now that you've identified a list of possible comforting items for your five senses, begin to collect those items or keep them handy for use in stressful moments.

The energy of estrangement is rich in possibility of how it can be explored in therapy. If reconciliation is possible, the *Estrangement Energy Cycle* could end here. However, for some clients, their process does not end here, nor does it end in reconciliation, as we will see in the next chapter.

Grief and Loss   **10**

A N UNDERSTANDABLE REACTION TO estrangement is grief and loss. Some women start grieving through the anticipatory grief process during the questioning stage of the *Estrangement Energy Cycle*. Others will feel the brunt of loss in this stage, as it comes after estrangement has been chosen and enforced. Grief and loss can manifest in many forms, including emotions that come in waves that resemble Elisabeth Kübler-Ross's *Five Stages of Loss* (2014), including denial, anger, depression, bargaining, and acceptance.

Take Enid, for example. She had elected not to estrange from her mom but was feeling the pressure to choose between a relationship with her mom and a relationship with her grandma. When she allowed herself to fully feel the emotions of her predicament, she felt new anger at both her mom and grandma for the stress she was under, in addition to older anger connected to their marked absence during her childhood abuse.

Charlotte was on a journey of exploring reconciliation with her mom, Sandra. She expected feelings of caution and desired proof that Sandra was different. What Charlotte did not expect was a grief response to show up with Sandra's attempt at reconnection. Sandra's apology brought with it the trauma memories that Charlotte had worked so hard to pack away. She required additional support to mourn the loss of Sandra's apology at an earlier time in her life, which she believed could have resulted in a healthier relationship for Charlotte and her children.

Keisha was grappling with the reality of mother Jeanie not demonstrating a willingness to change. After a handful of attempts to set new boundaries with Jeanie, Keisha found herself pursuing estrangement due to Jeanie's ongoing temper and violence response to conflict. Keisha believed estrangement would feel far less painful than the roller coaster of hope and hurt she felt every time Jeanie discounted her feelings or denied her behavior as violent within their relationship.

Regina had been estranged for years prior to pursuing therapy. However, she too experienced a grief and loss response to the estrangement while immersed in her therapeutic work. This stemmed from recognizing the estrangement's permanence, due to her mom's active connection to Regina's abusers. Regina mourned the loss of the mother she wanted and very much needed, wishing for a mom who would choose her over the perpetrators of her abuse.

Cindy's unexpected death brought an additional wave of grief and loss for Kasey, who was grieving for her childhood self who didn't have the empathetic, warm mother she felt she deserved. Cindy's death represented a significant loss for Kasey, where Kasey's hopes of Cindy showing up as a loving mom in adulthood and coming to her with sincere apologies for all that happened earlier in Kasey's life, were never to be.

Kathryn's grief was revealed beneath the rage that was her armor, protecting her from the insensitivity of others. She learned in therapy that her rage response came with thoughts and feelings of being underappreciated and manipulated. If she felt either of these were true, she would lash out in anger to protect herself. Kathryn wasn't fully estranged from her mother when working on her anger in therapy. However, she knew she needed a new structure for holidays in how triggering they could feel when her mom didn't respond with a phone call or a desire to see Kathryn or her grandchild. After several hurtful holidays propelled her to change things, Kathryn was satisfied with her new routine of low-key activities, lots of rest, and a focus on connecting with her daughter in healthy ways. Not only did Kathryn feel less stressed and hurt at the holidays; her relationship with her daughter improved, with her daughter expressing how much she appreciated the change to holidays because it reduced her stress levels as well.

Summer was determined to never include her mom, Cher, in her holiday plans. Rather than allowing grief and anger to overtake her at the thought of how selfish she felt Cher had been, Summer chose to redirect her energy into creating holiday traditions with her chosen family for both her and her daughter to make meaningful memories. This served as a soothing balm in Summer's own grief and loss response, allowing her to continue to feel in control of her life, including who she let be a part of it.

Toni, on the other hand, felt pressure to include her mom in holiday plans. Her grief and loss response had been suppressed for years in not wanting to upset her mother further, worrying her actions would push her mom into a deeper depressive state. Toni was worried any perceived slight by her mom would result in Jan rejecting her, increasing Toni's sense of loss in a relationship that already felt cold and distant due to Jan's depression. Toni's resulting panic fed into her people-pleasing to make Jan happy at the holidays. With the help of therapy, Toni faced her grief and loss connected to childhood events that had been put on hold in response to Jan's depressive episodes. Toni was then able to identify and implement new boundaries with mom to prevent Jan's depression cycles from dictating Toni's future plans.

Nina felt her grief and loss response to estrangement show up several times a year in the form of binge eating. With help, she was able to recognize grief as an uninvited guest at trauma anniversaries, holidays, and her children's birthday celebrations. By recognizing grief's purpose for marking events that would normally have a mother's support and presence, Nina was able to honor her grief and loss in healthier ways, including movement, writing, and art when significant dates came up on the calendar.

Grief and loss are no strangers to the therapy space. In estrangement, they are key players for processing what could have been and what may never be in a ruptured mother-daughter relationship. However, this is not the end of the *Estrangement Energy Cycle*, nor is it the end of a woman's work to heal from the pain of their mother-daughter estrangement. Let's take a closer look at the therapeutic work embodied in the next stage, discovering sense of self.

Discovering Sense of Self   11

ONE OF OUR FAVORITE EXPERIENCES as mental health profession-als is the client epiphany. The ah-ha that serves to catalyze positive change. *The goosebumps moment.* The point where they embrace a new discovery or take a significant step in meeting their goals. After the heaviness of the grief and loss stage, the discovering sense of self phase is a welcomed, empowered place for clients to land. As Anderson (2018, p. 43) describes the transformation, "when we choose to focus on and heal our mother stories, we transform them from something that wears us out and causes us to suffer into something that is a source of wisdom, creativity, and peace." As we've witnessed, adult women's identities have been significantly challenged through estrangement from their mothers, and at this stage a new identity is forming. The clinical themes and tools to support a client's new sense of self after estrangement are abundant, with the following being just a few favorites:

- successful self,
- trauma personification,
- identity formation,
- sobriety versus recovery,
- compassionate touch,
- reconciled relationship,
- positive role model,
- professional helper, and
- safe space.

Successful Self

Kasey desperately wanted to feel more sure of herself as she neared nine months of sobriety. She was feeling stuck in her trauma work, discovering a visceral reaction to being labeled a victim of abuse. Through the therapeutic exercise of visualizing her successful self (see Exercise 11.1), she embraced a new, empowered label of being called a survivor. With this chosen language, Kasey unlocked a vivid visual of speaking on the TEDx stage about her journey and recovery from addiction and trauma. The more Kasey dropped into the image of herself on stage, the more we were able to strengthen the image with her tapping different parts of her body in reinforcement (see Exercise 14.1). This allowed for her to feel the positive emotions associated with the imagery, which remained a motivator to continue her recovery work.

Exercise 11.1.   **Successful Self-Visualization**

Step 1: Grab a piece of paper or download our handout at estrange mentenergycycle.com. Read through this script before following the steps as we encourage you to do this exercise with your eyes closed.

Step 2: The script:

Get into a comfortable position and take three deep breaths.

Clear your mind, imagining you are in a dark, calm room.

Begin to imagine an image of yourself, an image of success.

What do you look like in this room? How is your posture? What are you wearing? What is your face doing?

Allow the image to pan out in your mind's eye. Who is around you? What is around you in this image of success?

What are you feeling as you see this image of yourself?

Allow yourself to feel positive sensations throughout your body as you continue to breathe.

Take a snapshot—like on your phone—of this image in your mind's eye. What *word* would bring this image back into focus within your mind at another time?

Say that word out loud. How does it feel?

Write the word down.

Trauma Personification

Similar to the inner critic personification exercise, trauma personification (see Exercise 11.2) allows the client to pinpoint the most upsetting or disruptive element of their trauma and separate from it by giving it a personality all its own. Sometimes trauma appears as a person; other times it appears as an object or thing. For Kathryn, curiosity about her rage response helped her identify a deep attachment trauma with mom, who was the onlooker to Kathryn's verbal and emotional abuse by her grandfather. Kathryn was able to explore the emotions associated with this hurt and personify them, including locating where they lived in her body. Kathryn's personification revealed a spiny, heavy, black mass on her back that curled her shoulders and constricted her breathing under its weight. She was then able to take this image into her EMDR work as one of her targets for further processing.

EXERCISE 11.2.   **Trauma Personification**

Step 1: Have a piece of paper and pen nearby or download our handout at estrangementenergycycle.com. Get into a comfortable position and close your eyes or put them at rest (e.g., looking down). Bring your attention inward and allow yourself to get curious about your trauma. What piece feels most distressing? What sensations are associated with it? What imagery? What name or phrase captures the trauma element or event? Write down what you are noticing.

Step 2: When you are ready to contain the trauma between moments of reflection or therapeutic work, visualize a container. Visualize placing it in the container, focusing on the container size, material, and shape. Once your trauma personification is successfully inside the container, visualize sealing it and placing it somewhere safe to allow your mind, body, and emotions to regulate. Note your container location on your piece of paper for future reference.

Identity Formation

Keisha had grieved the loss of a healthy, nonviolent mother significantly in the grief and loss stage, especially as she learned she was pregnant with her third child. She wished to overhaul her identity in the hopes of showing up as her best self for her children. Keisha began this process by exploring her response to the question, "who am I?" (see Exercise 11.3). This exercise allowed movement into strengths, barriers, and supports, forming the foundation for her next chapter of personal identity development.

EXERCISE 11.3.   **Who Am I Reflection**

Step 1: Grab a piece of paper or download our handout at estrange mentenergycycle.com. By drawing lines, cut the piece of paper into four (4) quadrants. In the top left quadrant, write "I am." In the top right quadrant, write "I want." In the bottom left quadrant, write "My blocks," and in the bottom right quadrant, write "My solutions."

Step 2: Fill out each box with what comes to mind. Ask yourself questions like, "What are my roles? What adjectives describe me? What do I want from my relationships, my career, and my personal life? What is blocking me from achieving my goals? What are my possible solutions to rid myself of these blocks?"

Step 3: Notice any themes within the quadrants or any emotions that show up in completing this exercise. If you are still struggling with answers to your blocks and solutions boxes, who can support you in making progress?

Sobriety Versus Recovery

Nina was managing to ride the waves of grief as each trauma anniversary came and went. She felt that she was finally putting the estrangement from her mother behind her, and discovered renewed energy to take better care of herself. Imagine her surprise when she sought the care of a medical professional and was treated like an addict. Nina knew that she had been labeled unfavorably more than a decade before in seeking pills as solace from her family conflict in addition to binge eating. Yet she wasn't prepared for the poor treatment of the medical community who responded to her as if she remained untrustworthy and believed her to be pill-seeking. Deeply hurt and ashamed, Nina found herself identifying another piece of herself to bring back to therapy in order to examine her current identity. She engaged in the self-portrait exercise (see Exercise 11.4), exploring the implications of sobriety versus recovery for choices in her past and present.

EXERCISE 11.4.   **Self-Portrait Exercise**

Step 1: Grab a blank piece of paper or download our handout at estrangementenergycycle.com. Begin by sketching out a head and torso for your self-portrait. Artistry is not the goal here so don't let your perfectionism get the best of you!

Step 2: Inside the torso of your drawing, write words that describe the roles you hold (e.g., wife, mother, daughter, artist, employee, volunteer).

Step 3: Inside the head of your drawing, write words that describe any anxieties and worries you have, such as your relationship with your mother, your productivity, your abilities as a parent, burnout, depression, or being overworked.

Step 4: Around the outside of the torso in your drawing, write words to describe you including your physical features, values, personality characteristics, and adjectives as desired.

Step 5: Around the outside of the head in your drawing, write words that capture what you need from others, such as compassion, understanding, space, hugs, distraction, affection, time to yourself, or reassurance.

Step 6: Review the final self-portrait, exploring key words that stand out or hold the most power over you in this moment. Grab some colored pencils, crayons, or colored pens and shade in the torso and head if you like. Focus on shading your drawing from left to right for bilateral stimulation and deeper processing as you continue your reflection of who you are and how you show up in the world.

Compassionate Touch

Enid found herself struggling with the past as well. By pursuing a safe space in therapy, she had finally faced the childhood molestation head-on, but continued to struggle with misplaced feelings of responsibility for what happened. This, combined with instances where she recoiled from her boyfriend's touch, had her worried that she would never feel comfortable in her own skin again. Enid was a great candidate for the compassionate touch exercise (see Exercise 11.5). Not only did this help her discover what touch felt safe or comforting to her, it helped her drop more into her body. She learned that practicing self-compassion in the form of phrases or words conveying gentleness and encouragement began to help her heal from her childhood wounds.

EXERCISE 11.5.   **Compassionate Touch Exercise**

Step 1: Grab a piece of paper or download our handout at estrange mentenergycycle.com. Begin by getting into a relaxed and present position, most likely seated, with feet flat on the floor and hands placed gently in your lap. Take several deep breaths.

Step 2: Begin an experiment with touch, starting with your dominant hand on neutral parts of your body. This might mean clasping your other hand, touching your feet, or resting your hands on your knees. Notice any sensation that arises from this touch.

Step 3: Continue exploration of compassionate touch, including holding your arms in a self-hug; touching your face, the top of your head, or the back of your neck; or placing your hands over your heart. Make note of which touch feels most comforting or evokes feelings of warmth for you. Also note which touch is not a good fit in feeling charged or uncomfortable.

Step 4: Recall a criticism or stressor and make note of any uncomfortable sensations in your body. Engage in your chosen compassionate touch as you continue to recall a criticism or stressor. Notice how your body and mind respond to the compassionate touch in the face of anxiety or worry, reinforcing any alleviated sensations or movement toward warmth and relaxation due to the compassionate touch.

Reconciled Relationship

Charlotte had worked hard to approach the possibility of reconciliation with her mom, Sandra, from a grounded, logical place. Yet every time she prepared to speak with Sandra on the phone, anxiety would surface, telling her that Sandra was going to hurt her again and that all the progress Sandra had made was a lie. Charlotte required additional skills beyond her five senses coping kit to remain present and willing to engage her mom on the phone. Charlotte was willing to try power poses (see Exercise 11.6) to reinforce feelings of being confident and in control. She would select a pose to try for a few minutes before a scheduled call and would move between poses during each call, in order to remain in her body in a self-assured, grounded way.

EXERCISE 11.6.   **Power Poses (Courtesy of Amy Cuddy)**

Step 1: Grab the script and an audio file for download at estrange mentenergycycle.com. Select a flat surface free of obstacles for standing or modify the poses for a sitting position if desired.

Step 2: Select one of three power poses below. Hold your selected power pose for at least two minutes. Breathe deeply and notice your strength and balance in this pose. Hold this power pose for as long as you feel comfortable.

Power Pose #1 V for Victory

Stand with your feet shoulder-width apart and raise your arms into a V position above your head. Keep your shoulders down and breathe through your belly, inhaling through your nose, exhaling out your mouth.

Power Pose #2 Wonder Woman Pose

Stand with your feet shoulder-width apart and put your fists on your hips. Feel your chest open up and breathe through your belly by inhaling in through your nose, exhaling out your mouth.

Power Pose #3 Open Pose

Stand with your feet shoulder-width apart and bring your hands up, elbows at your waist. Your hands will be palm up like an open yoga pose. Breathe through your belly by inhaling through your nose, exhaling out your mouth.

Positive Role Model

Summer had developed a level of confidence before entering therapy in having navigated estrangement from a young age. Her biggest worry, aside from running into mom Cher unexpectedly, was how her anxiety was impacting her own young daughter. Summer struggled to slow down and be still, making some therapeutic techniques a poor fit for her. Instead, Summer learned to embrace and hone her energy into mindful walking (see Exercise 11.7), a skill that could keep her present and grounded while still being on the move. Mindful walking was compatible with her tasks of raising a child and completing college and graduate school as a single mother. With each successful personal and professional milestone, Summer felt she was solidifying her identity as a positive role model for her daughter and her community.

EXERCISE 11.7.   **Mindful Walking**

Step 1: Grab the script and an audio file for download at estrange mentenergycycle.com. Select a flat surface free of obstacles for walking, either indoors or outdoors.

Step 2: Take several deep breaths as you straighten your spine, imagining a pole coming out the crown of your head that elongates your neck, spine, and torso. Take several more deep breaths, noticing any shift in your breathing by adopting this upright posture.

Step 3: Begin to notice your feet. As you prepare to lift one foot to begin walking, become aware of your muscles shifting, balancing the movement of your body weight as you lift your foot.

Step 4: As you proceed to lift one foot to begin walking, embrace an exaggerated slowness, as if you are moving in slow motion. Without losing your balance, notice the muscle groups that activate as you begin to walk, including the lifting of your foot, bending of your knee, balancing on one foot, and placing your foot on the ground in a stepping motion, heel to toe.

Step 5: Repeat these slow-motion movements as you walk, noticing how your body uses muscle and balance as it moves. Continue your walking with relaxed belly breaths and a straight, strong spine.

Step 6: As you finish your mindful walking, what do you notice in yourself? Is there a burst of energy? Increased oxygen? An improved flow to your breathing?

Professional Helper

Toni had worked diligently in therapy to identify her warning signs for backsliding into an unhealthy caregiver role with her mother, Jan. Although she recognized patterns of people-pleasing as a concern, she was adamant about the importance of maintaining a helper role as part of her identity. Toni was encouraged to explore the elements of the helping professions that could honor the part of her that wanted to help others. This exploration, combined with her personalized wellness recovery action plan (WRAP; see Exercise 11.8) to avoid burnout, left Toni feeling empowered to pursue a medical degree to hone her skills as an effective helping professional.

EXERCISE 11.8.   **Wellness Recovery Action Plan (WRAP)**

Step 1: Grab a piece of paper or download our handout at estrange mentenergycycle.com. Create a table that is two boxes wide and four boxes long. Label the top left box "What does it look like when I'm well?" Label the top right box "What does it look like when I'm not well?" For the second row, label the left box "Warning Signs/Internal" and label the right box "Triggers/External." For the third row, label the left box "My Supports" and the right box "When things are breaking down." For the final row, label the left box "Plan of Action" and the right box "What do I need from others?"

Step 2: Fill out the boxes to the best of your ability as they relate to you and your experience. If you get stuck, you can ask someone close to you like a loved one or spouse about how you show up when feeling well versus unwell. We've also included some common responses from others in our handout available for download for further reflection.

Step 3: Share your discoveries about yourself with someone who can hold you accountable, specifically focusing on "Plan of Action" and "What do I need from others?" sections. The WRAP plan is meant to help you identify signs of decline and burnout while creating a path and plan toward wellness.

Safe Space

Regina's renewed conviction for remaining estranged from her mother felt bittersweet. On one hand, she was safe from threats and manipulation of family members who denied her abuse, including her perpetrators. On the other hand, she had lost her mother for good in this decision and lacked healthy mother figures when she started therapy. This absence was especially painful when experiencing trauma flashbacks of the abuse. Regina struggled to regulate or connect with others in meaningful ways when flashbacks were at their strongest. Fortunately, Regina enjoyed photography as a hobby and responded well to the safe space exercise (see Exercise 11.9), taking a mental snapshot of places that were comforting and relaxing for her to bring into focus when needed. This served as respite from the flashbacks and helped her transition into the present moment, in order to engage others within her chosen community in safe ways.

EXERCISE 11.9.   **Safe Space**

Step 1: Grab the script and an audio file for download at estrange mentenergycycle.com. Get into a relaxed position with your feet flat on the floor if sitting. Close your eyes or put them at rest, softening your gaze.

Step 2: Take several deep breaths as you allow yourself to relax and bring your attention inward. Begin to bring to mind an image of a place that feels safe. This place can be real or imagined.

Step 3: Focus on this safe space in all its detail. What are the sounds of this place? What can you smell? What can you taste, touch, and see?

Step 4: Notice how you feel in this space. If it begins to feel like anything other than relaxed, calm, happy, or safe, you may need to restart this exercise to identify another safe space.

Step 5: Once you have your safe space captured in vivid detail, choose one word that would represent this space, giving you access to it again in your mind. Try out the word by saying it in your mind or aloud. If it feels positive and reinforces the imagery of your safe space, write the word down.

The discovering sense of self phase can be an empowering one for both client and therapist. Not only does it help our clients develop a new, positive identity; it can help them embark on the next chapter in their relationship with themselves and others. Not surprisingly, it also helps clients feel primed and ready for the next phase of the *Estrangement Energy Cycle*, which is deeper work. This stage, for many, encapsulates core belief work and oftentimes focuses on a woman's trauma healing.

Deeper Work 12

I T'S HELPFUL TO DEFINE THE DEEPER WORK stage as identifying and exploring themes within your client's therapeutic work, both historically and at present. As professionals, we are tasked with assisting clients in further exploration and healing related to their estrangement, which can include addressing any trauma that remains disruptive or contributes to persistent feelings of dysfunction. Fortunately, through previous and current therapeutic work, a client's greater awareness and refined coping skills can help them take the next steps in healing from mother-daughter relationship rupture and resulting estrangement. Additionally, their efforts can set them up for success with the final stage of the *Estrangement Energy Cycle* when they are ready to proceed. Let's explore some common themes of the deeper work stage with our nine courageous clients.

Theme #1: What Happened Is a Part of Me, But Doesn't Define Me

A powerful reframe that some of our clients adopt is one where they acknowledge the trauma that has happened to them, but recognize they are not exclusively defined by it. This separation feels similar to the acceptance and commitment therapy (ACT) technique of thought diffusion (see Exercise 12.1). In thought diffusion, we identify and label a thought as a thought and then name we are noticing that thought, creating space and separation from a negative emotion that comes with that charged thought. For example, what do you notice when reading the following sentences or saying them out loud?

I'm a failure.

I'm noticing that I'm having the thought that I'm a failure.

Which one feels more charged and painful to you? For most, the first sentence holds all the power of getting punched in the stomach. The second feels more diluted by all the extra words, and helps us make a shift to the logical mind, making it an effective alternative. Several of my clients over the years have been able to embrace this technique in order to remove some of the power and painful punch of their thoughts or inner critic.

EXERCISE 12.1.   **Thought Diffusion**

(Grab the script and an audio file for download at
estrangementenergycycle.com.)

The script:

Step 1: Identify a negative thought about yourself.
Step 2: Identify the sensation in the body this thought creates.
Step 3: Say out loud: the negative thought.
Step 4: Say out loud: "I'm having the thought that . . ."
Step 5: Say out loud: "I'm noticing I'm having the thought that . . ."

Charlotte had shared her trauma history with several trusted people over the years, leaving her hopeful that it would be that much easier to tackle her residual trauma symptoms with EMDR in the therapy office. Her deeper work required that she remain curious about how her childhood trauma shaped her behaviors as an adult and mother, including her perfectionism and desire for control. Charlotte had initially thought healing from her trauma was as simple as celebrating that she was nothing like her mother when parenting her own children. However, Charlotte's next painful layer to address in therapy was exploring how her hypervigilance, perfectionism, and controlling behaviors, which arose from her past trauma, impacted her spouse and four children in the present.

Enid had accepted the connection between her childhood molestation and her current panic attacks. Her deeper work required that she take the compassionate touch or neutral touch she'd discovered for herself and communicate safe touch options to those who loved her. With grandma, this meant advocating for boundaries on what kind of touch was allowed and when it felt safe. For her mother, Enid was relieved to not have touch remain absent in their relationship. As for her boyfriend, this meant several vulnerable conversations about safe zones on her body during sex. With a lot of patience and healthy communication, Enid was eventually able to enjoy sex and intimacy with her boyfriend, remaining present in her body rather than being triggered and dissociated.

Kasey felt the risk of relapse more strongly when her mom, Cindy, died. She had been working hard on her trauma related to her six-year-old-self and the emotional repression she was subjected to within her family system, when grief and loss were suddenly added to the mix. Kasey had work to do around fully feeling her grief and loss response to her mom's death in all its intensity, after being told her emotions were too much as a child. This meant learning to grieve wholeheartedly without censoring her tears or anguish in therapy. It also meant learning how to safely contain (hold) emotions when not in the safety of her own space with the container exercise (see Exercise 12.2). Although it felt scary and overwhelming at first, Kasey was able to finally feel the full extent of her emotions in cathartic and healing ways. This reduced her relapse potential in no longer feeling the urge to suppress her emotions with alcohol.

EXERCISE 12.2.   **Container Exercise**

Step 1: Grab the script and an audio file for download at estrangementenergycycle.com. Get into a relaxed position with your feet flat on the floor if sitting. Close your eyes or put them at rest, softening your gaze.

Step 2: Take several deep breaths as you allow yourself to relax and bring your attention inward. Identify all the things you wish to contain, things that are upsetting or require containment in not feeling safe to process in this moment. These things may be represented as objects, words, or images.

Step 3: Imagine a container to put these items in. Focus on the size, shape, color, and texture of the container. Visualize placing each item in the container, one by one.

Step 4: Check that all the desired items are successfully in the container. Visualize sealing the container and identify a safe place to store it, either real or imagined. Complete the visualization by seeing the container in this safe place.

Theme #2: I Know and Trust Myself

A second theme that may show up in deeper work with adult women estranged from their mothers is the experience of being more self-aware and therefore more trusting of themselves. After being subjected to criticism, verbal attacks, and sometimes manipulation from their mothers, clients can come to therapy feeling disconnected or unsure of who they really are.

This was the case for Nina, who feared that the hurtful things her mother said about her over the years were somehow true. In addition to recognizing times when her inner critic was her own voice versus her mother's, Nina required deeper work to better understand the brain-body connection tied to her former coping skills of binge eating and pills. Through the internal family system (IFS) self-meditation (see Exercise 12.3), Nina was able to explore how her trauma manifested as stomach pain and nausea, two sensations she would normally misinterpret and dull with food and substances. Through IFS, Nina learned how to sit with the sensations in her stomach and explore her inner world, in order to heal and integrate traumatized parts of herself into who she was in the present moment.

Toni struggled with self-confidence as it related to her worth as a helper and as a human. She continued to question how effective she was, even when receiving accolades in her work as a professional in medicine. Toni's deeper work included removing mental blocks to seeing her strengths. This involved identifying her values, successes, and strengths as a person. Toni discovered that her struggle with receiving compliments stemmed from the surface-level praise associated with mom Jan's depression over the years. Having bolstered her boundaries with Jan, Toni was finally ready to show up more openly with others, including receiving acknowledgment and appreciation from others while existing in a place of healthy self-worth.

Regina often kept her true thoughts and feelings hidden under a shield of matter-of-factness. Her significant trauma history had stunted her emotional intelligence, and there were times she presented to her friends and spouse as either an angry teenager or a wounded, scared little girl. The pendulum of her emotional presentation tended to create conflict in her relationships, where the once assertive Regina struggled to make even the simplest decisions—like what to have for dinner—without collapsing into rage or tears. Regina's deeper work involved increasing her emotional intelligence, including learning how to read cues in herself and others that would encourage a compassionate

Exercise 12.3. **Internal Family Systems (IFS) Self-Meditation**

Step 1: Grab the script and an audio file for download at estrange mentenergycycle.com.

Step 2: Read the script from start to finish before attempting, or play the audio file; you will want to keep your eyes closed or at rest for this exercise.

Script:

Get into a relaxed position and take several deep breaths.
Close your eyes and go inside . . .
And begin by focusing on your body sensations . . .
Just noticing wherever your attention goes in your body . . .
And being in that sensation.

Whether it's a warmth in your hands . . .
A tingling in your face . . .
A pressure in your belly . . .
Or a tension in your shoulders . . .
Whatever it is, just be present with that sensation.

As time goes on, your attention may wander.
Bring it back to your body.
Even a different part of your body . . .
And allow yourself to be present with that sensation.

As you focus on your body, allow it to relax you . . . and take you deeper inside yourself.
Just continuing to be with your body . . . deepening into yourself.

And now focus your attention on your belly, the sensations in your belly.
Whether it's a fullness . . . or a softness . . . or a solidness . . .
Or just the rise and fall of your belly with each breath . . .

Whatever it is, just be present with the sensations in your belly . . .
And allow them to take you into that place in your inner awareness . . .
Anchoring you . . . in your belly . . . coming to a grounded, solid place inside yourself.

response instead of a dysregulated one, in the interest of preserving her chosen, healthy relationships.

Theme #3: I Can Change This Trauma Legacy for My Children

A final theme to note in the deeper work stage of the *Estrangement Energy Cycle* relates to the legacy or passing of trauma traits on to the next generation. As women work hard to understand their mother-daughter estrangement and the abuse or trauma that can precede it, they tend to voice concern about the impact on their children, especially if they have daughters. The concern is that they will unwittingly damage their daughters, causing the cycle to continue. It is often identified as anxiety; we as professionals can hold space for their worries and concerns while honoring their motivation to have something different and better for their kids.

Keisha was no exception to the goal of being a better mom in the face of trauma. As she shed her old identity of victim to violence by her mother's hand, Keisha recognized that she wanted her environment to feel and look as different as she felt. This involved removing clutter and items once gifted to her by her mother, as well as rearranging her living spaces to outwardly represent the differences she felt within herself. Her deeper work included defining the characteristics of a healthy parent–child relationship and pursuing meaningful relationships with her children through quality time with each of them.

Kathryn had discovered the power of quality time in slowing down and redefining her holiday traditions with her daughter. Having her anger better under control, Kathryn was ready to do the deeper work of embracing vulnerability. She was tasked with asking for feedback from her child as she entered her autonomous teenage years. It was at this stage of life where her teenager could share how Kathryn was coming across or showing up, often in a brutally honest fashion. As uncomfortable as it is to have someone hold up the mirror for our behavior, Kathryn needed to hear, see, and acknowledge her child's response to her efforts to disrupt the trauma legacy of the women in her family. Kathryn was able to receive confirmation that her daughter was developing in healthy, expected ways thanks to some meaningful conversations with her teenager where Kathryn remained regulated and present.

Summer had limited insight into how her emotions affected her daughter when starting therapy. She had operated at high anxiety for so long that she assumed her daughter wouldn't know the difference, especially because Summer managed to get a lot of things done and looked high functioning from the outside. Summer also prided herself on being nothing like her mother, so she felt confident that her daughter would not feel embarrassed by her in any way. Summer's deeper work required her to take a closer look at her anxious presentation and the link to her young child's functioning. Although difficult, she was able to pinpoint areas she could improve for her daughter, including healthy sleep hygiene routines for herself and her daughter such as a predictable bedtime routine and limiting screen time before bed. She was also tasked with regulating herself before picking her daughter up from school each day. As she found herself backsliding into chaotic productivity, she was gently challenged in therapy to explore the impact on her child, including identifying the telltale signs of her child's dysregulation that resulted from Summer's unconscious modeling.

Themes are a powerful tool in therapy for estrangement and beyond. They not only help our clients continue their self-discovery experiences but also can help clients move into the final stage of the *Estrangement Energy Cycle*, a stage called redefining self-worth.

Redefining Self-Worth 13

YOUR CLIENTS HAVE COMPLETED a significant amount of work related to their mother-daughter estrangement and find themselves moving energetically into the final stage of the *Estrangement Energy Cycle*, which involves redefining self-worth. As indicated by their progress, clients have demonstrated continual effort and perseverance to fully accept their estrangement status and resulting shifts in personal and professional identities. Now that their new identity is solidified and the deeper work has been done, they are propelled into an empowered place of redefining their self-worth. We've emphasized how clients go through a questioning of their worth in the estrangement process, wondering if they are lovable or worthwhile to their mothers prior to the relationship rupture. At this final stage, a woman can embrace a new narrative about her value and contributions in the world—a narrative that strengthens values, builds boundaries, and opens her up to creating healthy relationships with chosen family and friends—a narrative where a woman's worth isn't wrapped up in how mother sees her, but in how she sees herself.

For Charlotte, Keisha, Kathryn, and Summer, this meant seeing their own worth as mothers, to hold themselves in compassion and patience, and to acknowledge their efforts at parenting from a healthier, connected place. It meant learning to give themselves grace when they felt they were backsliding into a hurt or reactive response with their children. It also meant celebrating their efforts to break the cycle of hurt from mothers to daughters, generation after generation.

For Nina, Enid, and Regina, embracing their self-worth meant disconnecting from unhealthy relationships with family members in addition to mom. It meant grieving the loss of family, friends, or community members who chose not to hold space for their experience. It meant cutting out folks who judged them for their choice without wanting to know their story. It also meant cultivating new relationships that could honor their estrangement status, knowing it wasn't the only thing to define them.

For Kasey, redefining self-worth included being defined as an adult child who lost her mother too soon. It was learning to comfort herself in ways that mom could not. It involved being sober and speaking up for sobriety-safe spaces within her community. It also included healing her childhood trauma parts so that she could finally grow into her full, emotional, inspirational potential with others. Kasey went on to become a leader in her sobriety community, becoming a mentor to other women. She provided the unconditional positive regard she herself craved from her mom to those who felt rejected and judged in their addiction.

For Toni, this stage meant embracing her worth as a professional, a caregiver, and a change agent in medicine, to accept recognition without hesitation, to not let negativity dampen her achievements, and to be present for compliments and maintain a balance of helping others while also taking care of herself.

Inspirational things can and do happen when self-worth is defined apart from others. It isn't just about what we can do for others; it's about who we are as people. For these nine women, redefining self-worth meant showing up authentically and wholeheartedly in the world, with or without their mothers.

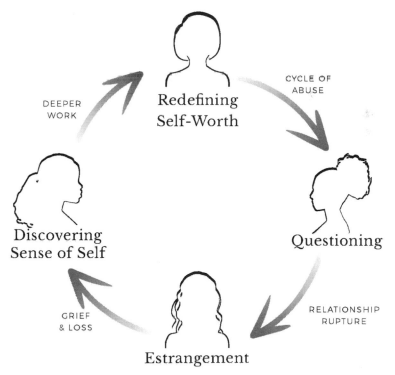

Estrangement Energy Cycle

Figure 14.1. The Estrangement Energy Cycle

LTHOUGH WE'VE COMPLETED OUR exploration of the *Estrange-ment Energy Cycle*, it's important to acknowledge that some clients will work through the cycle several times. Why might this be? One scenario would be when reconciliation with mother is reached and then boundaries are violated in a new, equally painful way—like for Keisha, who kept giving her mom, Jeanie, chance after chance, only to feel the hurt and relationship rupture again when Jeanie violated her trust or continued to accuse Keisha of competing with her for romantic partners. Or for Nina, who tried several times to repair things with her mom only to hit a breaking point, lashing out physically, and being charged with assault. It is completely human of us to have hope that our relationship with our mother will change for the better. Until we enter the *Estrangement Energy Cycle* and move through the stages, we may not even be aware of the emotional roller coaster that we are on with mom. Therefore, it is paramount that as mental health professionals, we meet our clients where they are. Our job continues to be about supporting them in self-discovery related to their relationship with mom, at their own pace and with no agenda from us.

Another scenario where the *Estrangement Energy Cycle* might be revisited with clients is when they connect to romantic partners or their chosen family who mirror the abuse cycles they've disrupted with mom. For Enid, this was indicated in a familiar, uncomfortable feeling with her grandma, who demanded she choose between mom or grandma to have a quality relationship. She was told she could have one but couldn't have both. Regina recognized some similarities between her family's abuse and her spouse's mistreatment of her when they were fighting. Although it can be painful to discover that we find ourselves again in a cycle where estrangement might be warranted, the therapy space is an appropriate place to process the circumstances that contribute to a client's current predicament, while providing zero judgment and heaps of compassion.

This brings us to our final clinical tool in support of a client's journey through estrangement and beyond. Emotional freedom technique (EFT) tapping (see Exercise 14.1) is another tool to regulate the nervous system through stimulation of various pressure points. What makes it feel easier than other tools for some is that there is no need to reframe our negative thoughts or emotions while engaging in the practice of it. Instead, a client names the thoughts and feelings as they tap the points in a pattern to notice any shifts within their body. For example, a client may voice something like, "I can't believe I'm in an abusive relationship again. I feel so embarrassed. Why do I keep doing this to myself?" As they hear their thoughts and feelings out loud, in tandem with the tapping, the emotional charge is reduced and they may find themselves naturally moving into cognitive reframes, such as "I've worked through this before; I can do it again. I'm aware of it now, so I can change things."

EXERCISE 14.1.   **Emotional Freedom Technique (EFT) Tapping**

Step 1: Download the diagram of tapping points at estrangement energycycle.com.

The total list of tapping points are

1. The heel of your hand
2. Your inner eyebrow
3. Your temple
4. The place where your undereye meets your cheekbone
5. The skin between your nose and your lip
6. The skin between your chin and your lip
7. Your collarbone
8. Your lowest rib at your side
9. The top of your head

Step 2: Identify any negative or charged sensations in your body as you recall your worries or stressors. Begin by tapping the heel of your hand with your opposite hand. Name out loud your worries or stressors, without censoring, reframing, or revising your word choice.

Step 3: Move down the list of tapping points as you express your emotions out loud. Allow your worries or thoughts to come to you as you tap.

Step 4: Complete three or more cycles of tapping as you move down the tapping points on your body. Notice any shifts in the negative sensations that were present at the beginning of the exercise. Notice which tapping spots you found most comforting or liked best. Repeat your tapping cycle as needed for the desired positive shift in sensations and emotions.

Change is the ultimate goal of estrangement, whether it be a change to the mother-daughter relationship for the better, or a separation and reworking of a woman's identity as an estranged daughter. This shared desire for change is why many women pursue therapy, if they have the means. As a woman completes this significant work, we might revisit the *Estrangement Energy Cycle* with her when celebrating her progress in therapy, such as at graduation or when planning a successful discharge from services. A personal favorite of mine is to ask clients to recall what things were like for them when they started therapy, in order to reflect on their progress and celebrate where they are now. Some clients struggle to remember the hardship in full detail if they are in a healthier, functional spot at present. Or perhaps they prefer to keep the pain in the rearview mirror. Helping them identify how far they've come, including walking through the stages of the *Estrangement Energy Cycle* and highlighting milestones and ah-ha moments they experienced along the way, can be a meaningful part of closure in your therapeutic work together.

Treating Men Who Are Estranged 15

ALTHOUGH THIS BOOK FOCUSES ON adult women and the estranged mother-daughter relationship, there is the possibility that you will treat men in your practice who are estranged. Estrangement for men can look different, including their presentation in the therapy office. For men, estrangement may bring up feelings of resentment, outrage, or anger versus the traditional emotions of sadness, guilt, and shame in women. This could be in part due to men not feeling the same kind of pressure to win their mother's approval or be in helpful or caregiving roles to parents the way women are expected to be. The common expectation for men is that they will grow apart from their mothers in seeking partners and creating families of their own.

We've also acknowledged that estrangement can occur for various reasons, including financial strain, relational conflict, mental health, and trauma. It's important to recognize that men may choose estrangement because of partners or spouses as well. Perhaps the partner or spouse is encouraging a man's estrangement from his mother in believing the mother-son relationship is unhealthy. A man may pursue estrangement if his family does not approve of his spouse, feeling that he must choose between them. He may justify estrangement for this reason, stating he no longer wants to hear the criticisms or slights he perceives are being made against his spouse or partner by his mother or both parents. Or a man can marry into wealth, resulting in him feeling he is at a different status than his family members, which causes him to limit contact with them.

A final area to emphasize is a gender difference observed by Agllias (2016) in her research on estrangement. Men and women respond differently in how they move toward acceptance of estrangement. Women tend to be more emotive in order to grieve and process the loss associated with estrangement, whereas men are more likely to respond with problem solving and intellectualizing what happened, in order to help them move on from an estranged relationship. There is also a societal expectation that men will "get over" things more quickly than women, which could include relationship rupture.

Lastly, men can move through the *Estrangement Energy Cycle* just like women, although their perceptions of themselves in the process can look a bit different. Be sure to honor their experiences and meet them where they are, just as we would any client going through the process of estrangement. Asking clarifying questions and helping them connect with their emotions can be impactful in helping men heal.

Clinical Competencies in Estrangement

16

WITH 1 IN 12 PEOPLE EXPERIENCING estrangement from at least one family member (Agllias, 2016), we, as professionals, can expect to encounter clients who want to explore or address their estrangement energy within a safe therapeutic environment. Now that we've explored the *Estrangement Energy Cycle* in depth, it's important not only to encourage ongoing self-assessment related to biases and expectations of estrangement but also to gauge our clinical competencies on this complex relationship dynamic. The clinical competencies assessment featured here is broken into three parts: assessment, professionalism, and intervention. Let's take a closer look at each part and the reasoning behind each question that has been included in this self-assessment, from a clinical lens. The full assessment can be viewed in Appendix D and can be downloaded for your use at estrangement energycycle.com.

Assessment

1. *Clearly asks about client relationships as part of case conceptualization.*
   If we don't ask about relationships and/or normalize the possibility of relationship conflict, clients may not disclose their estrangement status, which could be a missed opportunity to add context to current reported symptoms, as well as inform therapeutic treatment goals.
2. *Effectively gathers information on client relationship dynamics as they relate to the client's presenting concerns of estrangement.*

It's important to ask clarifying questions on a client's relationships, such as the current relationship status, closeness of each relationship, and asking clients who they confide in or seek support from, without assuming their chosen person is a family member.

3. *Identifies risk factors for estrangement from a trauma-informed perspective.*

   Remaining aware of the increased possibility of estrangement resulting from abuse, neglect, trauma, and ACEs is helpful for a clinician engaging a new client.

4. *Recognizes physical and emotional symptoms connected to estrangement energy.*

   Understanding estrangement symptoms and their impact on a client physically, emotionally, relationally, mentally, and spiritually prevents misdiagnosis or misaligned therapeutic goals.

5. *Identifies the client's current stage within the* Estrangement Energy Cycle.

   Recognizing each stage of the cycle is not only important for proper case conceptualization but also can serve as psychoeducation and normalization with clients in support of their ongoing reflection and treatment goal progression.

6. *Develops treatment goals that are appropriate for the client's current stage of estrangement.*

   Similar to recognizing each phase of the cycle, developing client-centered goals that are specific, measurable, attainable, realistic, and timely (SMART) is imperative to their healing. Treatment goals should reflect a client's desired outcomes, whether it be wish for reconciliation or pursuit of permanent estrangement.

7. *Remains knowledgeable about when to seek additional information from the client for added context and conceptualization.*

   Estrangement is a complex, painful process for both estranger and estrangee. Our ability as professionals to ask clarifying questions rather than assuming a client's experience with estrangement is vital to building rapport and trust within the therapeutic relationship.

8. *Incorporates cultural considerations from the RESPECTFUL model.*

   Estrangement does not discriminate. Cultural considerations remain an important aspect of working with estrangement as they relate to values, relationship expectations, and feelings of responsibility toward family. It's important to explore a client's possible internal battle between Western expectations of autonomy and independence versus Eastern expectations of remaining family focused and putting family needs before their own.

Professionalism

1. *Maintains appropriate boundaries with clients.*

    Boundaries are a significant focus of estrangement energy work and should be modeled between therapist and client as well. A therapist's ability to remain aware of the desire to rescue, "fix it," or adopt the maternal role is critical with estrangement clients.

2. *Remains aware of own biases and beliefs related to the family system and estrangement.*

    Holding our own beliefs, biases, and agendas in check is an important aspect of healthy boundaries and embodying a professional therapeutic relationship.

3. *Offers abundant compassion and zero judgment.*

    Compassion is a foundational element of helping women (and men) through estrangement energy and other therapeutic goals. Assumptions about their relationships and response to conflict are not invited into the therapy space. Allow clients to explore and define their experiences as uniquely their own.

4. *Adopts client-preferred language for estrangement experience.*

    Since estrangement remains stigmatizing for both estranger/adult child and estrangee/parent, invite the client to define their experiences in their own words. By adopting the same preferred language as the client, the clinician continues to model zero judgment and plenty of compassion for their experience.

5. *Avoids advice-giving or recommendations to reconcile or estrange.*

    Clients may be seeking therapy to get an expert opinion on their relationship with their parent. Avoid the trap of giving advice! Rather, reassure the client that they are the expert in their own lives and you, as the professional, are here to support them in identifying their next steps.

6. *Identifies countertransference and seeks support when necessary.*

    Even as professionals, we are human first (Castro Croy, 2022). If a client's experience mirrors your own or you find yourself triggered or struggling for neutrality, seek supervision or consultation.

7. *Pursues additional education, consultation, or supervision when needed.*

By no means do mental health professionals have to have all the answers when it comes to a client's estrangement energy journey. By seeking education, training, resources, and professional support, a clinician can feel more confident that they are doing their therapeutic best for their clients.

Intervention

1. *Forms a collaborative, working relationship with the client that includes rapport.*

Recognizing that estrangement signifies a grief and loss experience for many, building rapport and trust with the client is foundational to their ability to engage in meaningful work within the therapeutic space.

2. *Provides psychoeducation on attachment, trauma, and estrangement as appropriate.*

Part of the therapeutic work is normalizing some of the client's experiences through psychoeducation, compassion, and storytelling when appropriate. For some clients, knowing they aren't the only one navigating estrangement energy, that they are not dysfunctional or alone in their experience, is reassuring.

3. *Identifies different therapeutic tools congruent with the client's current stage of the* Estrangement Energy Cycle.

An indicator of a competent, confident therapist is their ability to introduce therapeutic tools that address a client's symptoms and challenges in the present, while supporting long-term goal progression as well.

4. *Adapts therapeutic interventions to be culturally relevant and compatible for client work.*

In having built rapport and completed a thorough assessment, the mental health professional can remain mindful of interventions that are respectful and appropriate for a client's lived experience, based on their disclosures.

5. *Requests feedback from the client on the therapeutic process to support goal progression.*

Although it can feel vulnerable, asking a client for feedback on their experience in therapy reduces the therapist-is-the-authority power dynamic. It also increases collaboration and models transparency of naming challenges in the therapy space, which can then be addressed in an empowered, therapeutically appropriate way.

Now that we've uncovered a richer context for the clinical competencies listed above, how would you respond to each question? Has your level of competency shifted from the beginning of the book to this point in the reading? Consider revisiting these competencies from time to time to gauge your progress as a professional.

When Someone You Know
Is Estranged

17

ONE OF THE MORE COMMON QUESTIONS I get as a professional is how to respond to a person who discloses their estrangement from their mother (or both parents). Imagine you're at a work dinner attempting to make polite conversation, so you embark upon the topic of family. Instead of it being a neutral topic as you hoped, you watch the person across from you start to shut down, get angry, or fight tears. Or perhaps you are in the process of getting to know a new dating partner who shares that they are estranged and you don't know what to ask or say next! Conversations about family can be tough for all parties in an estranged relationship. Therefore, it's a question I appreciate from community members as a therapist, because it shows people care and are trying to be thoughtful to the person who is living with estrangement. Let's explore some common questions and experiences for support persons of an adult daughter (or son) who is estranged.

For Partners

Recognizing how painful the process of estrangement can be for your loved one, here are some things to consider as the compassionate partner or spouse of a person who has experienced a relationship rupture with their mother.

1. *Know That the Holidays Can Be Heavy*

    Holidays are challenging for folks for a variety of reasons. This might include family conflict, death, trauma anniversaries, and toxic relationships. When it comes to estrangement, the cultural expectation of holidays being focused on family can feel ostracizing to an estranged person. If your partner is not currently connected to family but is subjected to movies, advertisements, and events catered to holiday family fun, they can experience additional or elevated grief and loss.

Recall how Kathryn dreaded the holidays? If she felt obligated to go see her mother, the trip always ended with her feeling stressed, financially taxed, and inevitably in a verbal fight with either her mother or her daughter by the time the visit was over. Kathryn had learned how holidays themselves could trigger her rage because of the absence of healthy family members who could make an effort to be a part of her life. Through difficult trauma work, she came to embrace a new definition of holidays spent at home, creating meaningful traditions that reduced the stress placed on both her and her daughter.

2. *Recognize That the Body Remembers*

Trauma events have a way of sticking with us, not just in our memory but at a deeper, cellular level as well. As a therapist, I've had dozens of clients over the years come into sessions reporting they felt symptoms of depression, dread, anxiety, or loss seemingly out of the blue and couldn't pinpoint why. When I asked them if there was any significance to the season, month, or day, oftentimes they would identify a trauma they hadn't consciously tracked, but that still had a tremendous impact on them, such as a family member's death, a car accident, sexual assault, suicide, or natural disaster. They weren't actively recalling these events, but their body remembered and responded by recreating some of the emotions or sensations associated with the trauma.

Remember how Nina's body would signify trauma anniversaries through a sudden low mood and increased body aches and pains? She is not alone in having her body remember significant and traumatic moments in her life. By learning to recognize the warning signs in her body and plan ahead, Nina could feel more regulated in how she wanted to respond to these markers of trauma. She felt empowered to experiment with days of rest versus working through a difficult period by focusing on something structured and productive. Having the choice on trauma anniversaries made her feel more in control of her body and emotions.

3. *Acknowledge Cultural Expectations of Family*

In addition to holidays being heavy, a cultural expectation of the importance of family can increase your loved one's feelings of shame or guilt about their estrangement from their mother. This occurs because of messages about the importance of family such as "family comes first," or accusations of adult children being selfish and dishonoring their family by straying from their family's values or sphere of influence. Additionally, your loved one might interact with a person who reiterates these messages, arguing that they should reconcile with their mother or risk significant regret, such as when their mother dies. Cultures that emphasize family over individuals can bring up self-doubt in your loved one about not trying hard enough to repair the relationship, or can intensify feelings of failure that they weren't successful in healing the relationship with their mom. It's important to recognize how, every day, normed portrayals of family can be triggering for your loved one in not having that expected dynamic.

Toni was a person who felt pressure to be around her family members out of obligation to them. Even though her mother's depression had a negative impact on Toni's mental health, she subjected herself and her spouse to regular interactions because of childhood messages that family is the most important thing in a person's life outside of being helpful to others. Toni had a lot to rework regarding her internal messages of worth being connected to caregiving and people-pleasing.

4. *Follow Your Partner's Lead*

When walking into a scenario where discussions of family systems or dynamics come up, allow your partner to lead the conversation. Support them in their decision to disclose as much or as little as they need to in order to interact with others in ways that feel safe to them. If they decide to not disclose their estrangement, they have their reasons. If they choose to name their current status as an adult estranged from a parent, that's their choice too. Showing up in solidarity for whatever response might come next from others will help your loved one feel supported by you, especially if the other person's response is unsympathetic, argumentative, or unintentionally hurtful.

Enid's boyfriend caught on quickly as to how uncomfortable Enid felt talking about her family. When it came time for her to meet his parents, he encouraged her to share whatever she wanted, reassuring her that his family had no intentions of prying into her personal life but, rather, wanted to get to know her as someone important enough for him to bring home to visit. Enid was able to develop a new level of self-awareness from noticing what she chose to share with her boyfriend's family. Experimenting with what to disclose without oversharing, she realized she no longer wanted to remain avoidant and stuck between her mother and her grandma.

5. *Ask, "What Do You Need?"*

When your partner or loved one finds themselves triggered by people, places, media portrayals, or memories, there is one powerful question you can ask them as their partner. Couples' therapists would agree with me when I say this question has saved relationships! Try asking your loved one, "what do you need?" Or ask, "what do you need in this moment?" These questions can be especially helpful because they give your partner permission to advocate for what might help them best. Perhaps they want a hug or to be left alone. Maybe they want to brainstorm or are asking for your help to fix things. Oftentimes, they actually just want to vent by expressing their thoughts and emotions in ways that leave them feeling seen by you as someone they trust.

It was rare for Summer to mention her mom much, even with her partner of six years. Yet every once in a while she would come to him upset, having heard from family or seen something on social media that indicated Cher was still living the partying lifestyle. This information would trigger Summer's anger, which her partner learned to respond to with empathy, asking her what she needed in these moments that could honor her feelings. Typically, she wished to vent to someone who knew her well in order to express her outrage, anger, and hurt at Cher's choices. Thanks to him holding space for this cathartic release of emotions oftentimes deeply buried, Summer felt she could re-regulate and resume her life.

6. *Encourage Chosen Connections*

As a partner, it's not expected that you be the one and only support person to your loved one. It's not fair to them and it's not healthy for you. Putting all of our needs on one person is a recipe for disaster because it can result in inequality, resentment, codependency, and burnout. Therefore, it's recommended that you encourage your partner to develop additional healthy relationships, including some with parental figures if appropriate. Similar to folks who describe their chosen family as people who love and respect them, can your loved one cultivate this kind of relationship with another mother-like or father-like figure? Can they lean on friends, colleagues, mentors, or family members as needed? Chosen connections such as these can have healing qualities for an estranged person. By exploring and building their support network alongside them, your loved one will feel they have options without over-relying on any one person, including you.

Keisha was feeling overwhelmed by her latest pregnancy and understood that her boyfriend felt obligated to work as much as possible before the baby arrived. Knowing that leaving her alone with her thoughts could be damaging, he encouraged her to connect with other moms and maternal figures in the hopes that she wouldn't feel lonely or isolated. Keisha was able to connect with a couple of moms at a kids' clothing swap, including several moms with multiple kids like herself. One parent in particular was an older mom who bonded with Keisha in ways that were healing for her estrangement from her mother. Through these connections, Keisha was able to lean on other moms during her pregnancy and discovered a new passion for thrifting and repurposing, which allowed her to design a nursery that brought her a lot of joy on a little budget.

For Parents

The process of estrangement can be equally painful for parents. Fortunately, there are several books available to take a deeper dive into the reconciliation process or that focus on healing from permanent estrangement with your adult child. Check out the following books written for parents:

- *Rules of Estrangement* by Joshua Coleman (2021);
- *Done with the Crying* by Sheri McGregor (2016); and
- *Estrangement of Parents by Their Adult Children*, revised second edition by Sharon Waters (2019).

Readiness for Reconciliation

Something frequently discussed in various books on estrangement is the possibility of reconciliation. You want to reconcile with your adult child, so what do you need to consider or do to make that happen? Consider the following tough questions regarding your readiness to reconcile:

1. *Why do you want to reconcile?* Being honest with yourself is the first step. Do you want to repair the relationship? Do you want to feel heard and validated in your choices? Are you looking to get even? Do you want a relationship with your grandchildren? There are any number of reasons why a parent wants to reconcile, and being prepared with a response for yourself and your estranged adult child should they ask would be an important first step.

2. *What are your expectations of the reconciled relationship?* As humans, it's not uncommon to hear folks say they want everything to go back to the way it was, or to start over, both of which would be problematic for the estranger/adult child who made this choice reflecting that something wasn't right. Going backward or to sameness would be a significant issue for them. What do you want the reconciled relationship to look like? Recognize that the relationship could be better or worse, but most likely just different.

3. *What steps will you agree to for reconciliation?* As you attempt to reengage your adult child, what offerings or compromises can you accept? Are you open to phone calls to start? Are you willing to have a relationship with your daughter-in-law but not speak to your estranged son? Are you pursuing a relationship with your grandchildren, even if it means you aren't on speaking terms with their mother? Knowing your own boundaries in the reconciliation process will help both you and your adult child navigate the testing phase of reconciliation.

4. *What can you take responsibility for?* In other words, have you done your own reflection of what happened? Are you prepared to accept your adult child's accusations and avoid arguing? Can you clearly name the offending actions prior to estrangement being pursued? Are you clear on the priority being repairing the relationship over determining whose memories of events are right?

Several authors say reconciliation is possible by owning your behavior and acknowledging your adult child's experience. Although it's tempting, arguing about the accuracy of their memories of trauma or abuse isn't helpful. This is their experience as they know it. Even though you may remember something completely different, arguing about what happened will further drive the wedge between you and your adult child. Instead, consider family therapy. Consider focusing on the future instead of the past. Be accepting of their hurt and resulting caution in wanting to take it slow to see if the relationship is mendable. Be prepared for tests from them to determine your truthfulness and authenticity. Agllias (2016, p. 63) states that "after long periods of estrangement, they [adult children] need to go back to the relationship to test their reality or perception of previous events and assess the potential for reconciliation." Coleman (2021) and McGregor (2016) emphasize that reconciliation can take years.

Kasey leaned into additional therapy sessions when her mom, Cindy, died unexpectedly. She felt she needed to come to terms with the realization that her mom would never come to her with an apology or offer to reconcile. Until Cindy's death, Kasey had maintained a fantasy that her mom would suddenly realize how hurtful she had been and come to Kasey, hugging her and apologizing for all that had happened while promising to be a better mom. Kasey spent several therapy sessions grieving the loss of this possibility, including examining all the things she had hoped could have been different with her mom in order to repair their relationship.

Parent Dynamics

Another question that comes up is about when one parent is still talking to their estranged adult child. Is this a good idea? In my experience, it's rare to have one parent in contact with their estranged adult child because of the assumed unification between parents who are still in a committed relationship with one another. Your estranged child might worry that their information will be shared with the parent they are choosing not to be in contact with. The experience of one parent being talked to by an estranged child may be more common with divorced parents because your lives are separate. In this situation, an adult child might feel it is safer to connect with one parent without the risk of information being shared with the other without their consent.

Regina reconnected with her dad when she became an independent adult living outside her mother's household. She felt it was safe to speak to him because of the divorce from her mother so many years prior and their lack of communication as a result. Her mom and her dad were not on speaking terms thanks to her stepdad, so Regina felt motivated to track him down with minimal risks to the current estrangement from her mom. Unfortunately, not long after their reconnection, her dad was diagnosed with cancer and died within months of his diagnosis. Regina was devastated by the loss of her dad but valued what limited time they had, stating she was glad she had reconnected with him to prove to herself that she could build a healthy relationship with a parent before he passed.

Shared Grief

It may be difficult to imagine that your adult child is experiencing their own grief and loss reaction in response to the estrangement, but they are. Although they may look calm, even relieved, Agllias (2016), author of *Family Estrangement: A Matter of Perspective*, shares that survey respondents indicate similar grief responses and symptoms to the shared estrangement status, including anticipatory grief when considering the decision to estrange, and posttraumatic stress symptoms for weeks or months after. Adult children report symptoms of sadness, helplessness, anger, and shock when choosing estrangement. Unlike grief and loss as the result of a family member's death, there isn't a sense of finality or closure when it comes to grief associated with estrangement. This experience of grief emphasizes how difficult the decision to become estranged from a parent can be, especially when the adult child indicates they are having to choose between several hard choices to protect their physical or mental health.

Nina felt her grief and loss response as crushing waves of emotion throughout adulthood when thinking of her estrangement from her mother. Although she had maintained the estrangement for several years, certain events or holidays left her in tears, hiding away in her bed with the wish to sleep through difficult memories and the self-doubt, guilt, and shame associated with her estrangement status. It took Nina leaning into her grief to fully understand what the highs and lows of emotion meant for her healing process. From there, she realized that much like an ocean wave could feel like it was drowning her, she had to trust and tread water in response to difficult emotions, knowing they would eventually recede.

Supporting Self-Awareness

A significant part of reconnecting with your adult child *or* healing and moving toward acceptance of the estrangement is doing your own work. How can you gain clarity on the parts you played in the relationship rupture? What contrasting evidence do you have for healthy familial relationships? Where can you bridge the gaps to show up as your healthiest, authentic self for possible reconciliation? What reframes can you discover in the estrangement to help you heal? Agllias (2016) describes the pursuit of enhanced self-awareness as a critical part of the process of learning how to live with estrangement. Although we can't predict the final outcome of your efforts, the hope is that any self-awareness work you complete will benefit you at this stage of your life, regardless of the final relationship status with your adult child.

Charlotte's mom, Sandra, wanted to prove to her that she had changed. She had asked to talk on the phone, hoping Charlotte would give her a chance. When Charlotte made the decision to call her back, Sandra was ready and willing to acknowledge her part in the trauma that Charlotte had suffered and shared openly all the things she had done to improve herself and her life. Sandra was proud to share how she'd discovered mindfulness and meditation, hoping it could be a skill that brought her and Charlotte together when exploring and healing from past events.

Another strategy to consider in your own estrangement healing is to recall the positive qualities or memories of your adult child's younger years. Although you may not be speaking at present, which is incredibly painful, can you feel more connected to them by recognizing the values you both share, like our four-generations-estranged family mentioned earlier in this book? One task they could each embark on during their estrangement status was finding that shared value. In their case, the value was a never-wavering commitment to their spouses, regardless of what their family members thought of them. Instead of focusing on being angry that they were not on speaking terms, several parents were able to uncover respect for their estranged family members who had conveyed a strong message of loyalty and commitment to their partners or spouses, in response to scrutiny or judgment by the family. Parents found themselves admitting this response was admirable because they, too, would feel compelled to defend and align with their spouse or partner as well.

One of my younger clients stands out to me as a second example to illustrate this concept. She had processed immense verbal abuse and neglect at the hands of her father when she was a child and had worked hard to find a level of acceptance that would reduce her posttraumatic stress symptoms. In one particular session, she was reflecting on all her father's character flaws, naming how she was determined never to be like him. In having solid rapport, I knew I could challenge her by asking what positive or neutral qualities he could have passed on, that she was willing to accept. With almost no hesitation, she named his loyalty to his friends as acceptable and compatible with her current loyalty to her friends. Although surprised, she was able to acknowledge that she had, in fact, found one value they could share despite her father's flaws.

As a parent of an estranged adult child, you are riding waves of uncertainty. Coleman (2021) encourages you to reach out to your adult child by letter to attempt to reengage and support reconciliation. However, knowing that this effort isn't always successful, perhaps you choose to focus on healing for yourself. In her revised second edition, Waters (2019) expands on ideas for positive coping for parents who are estranged, including but not limited to

- pursuing healthy distractions,
- embracing movement,
- getting outside,
- taking a trip,
- mentoring,
- writing or journaling,
- cuddling your pets, or
- volunteering.

By cultivating your own coping kit of things that help you find meaning in your life, not only can you adjust to the estrangement in your own time; it can also provide a new perspective. Your efforts to reflect and grow from the estrangement can be empowering, while also supporting reconciliation efforts with your adult child should they choose to reengage you to explore repairing the relationship.

For Siblings

A strained relationship between mother and daughter can ripple out to siblings as well. Siblings may feel that they are caught in the middle, wanting to please both parties and maintain connection to both. Or they could feel pushed to choose sides, aligning with one and becoming estranged from the other as a natural consequence. This can be a heart-breaking occurrence for you as the sibling, as well as the estranged child who is now grieving the loss of both a parent and a brother or sister.

Should you choose to walk the delicate line of maintaining relationships with both your mother and your sister, here are some ideas to keep your boundaries healthy with both.

1. *Don't Share What They Share*

    The urge to share with your sibling what mom is saying about your sibling is strong. However, this information can be very hurtful to your sibling, who is attempting to achieve a clean break from that relationship. Your disclosures can intentionally or unintentionally keep the trauma cycle alive by giving them a play-by-play of what mom is saying. The reverse is also true, where you share what your sibling is saying or doing with a parent who is estranged. Not only does this keep the wounds raw for your parent, who is trying to grapple with feelings of abandonment and rejection within their family system; your sibling may feel betrayed by your sharing of information they believed was shared with you in confidence. In summary, don't share information that is shared with you. It was meant for you and for you only.

2. *Don't Attack Their Character*

    When a sibling or parent attempts to vent to you about the estrangement, it's not uncommon for them to want you as an ally. This is not an invitation to attack the character of the other party. Allow your loved one to vent without taking sides. If they force the issue, clearly and confidently state that you care about them, which is what you want to stay focused on rather than taking sides. It is also not your responsibility to defend either side or their choices that resulted in estrangement.

3. *Attempt to Remain Neutral*

    Recognizing that you may only see one piece of the puzzle in the conflict between mother and daughter, attempt to remain neutral around the details of the estrangement. Even if you were raised alongside your sibling and feel that you witnessed all the same events, trauma cements different memories for different people. Your experience is not their experience. Arguing or defending one perspective as the "true perspective" will result in further distance from your sibling if you aren't careful.

4. *Reflect Their Emotions*

   Instead of getting caught up in the details, remain focused on your sibling's emotions. By reflecting their hurt, anger, or outrage, you keep the focus on them and their needs rather than the details of the conflict. They may disclose a variety of emotions, all of which are valid. Acknowledge without attempting to minimize or negate their emotions. Statements such as "I can see how that hurt you," or "I hear how painful this is for you," can indicate that you are listening with compassion.

5. *Don't Be a Mediator*

   It's a delicate balance of empathy and compassion when listening to your sibling speak of the estrangement. You are at risk of triangulation in being connected to both your sibling and your parent, and you will want to avoid being the messenger between both parties. You may find yourself taking on the role of mediator in wanting them to reconcile. After all, they are your family and you want everyone to get along. The desire to reconcile is yours to own. Avoid allowing hope to push you into the "fix-its" where you attempt to repair the relationship for them.

6. *Have Your Own Support*

   You are human, and the desire to have an intact, healthy family is natural. However, watching your family members go through an estrangement can take its toll on you as well. Consider having your own support outside of your family. This could be a mentor, mental health professional, or friend who can remain neutral to your circumstance while allowing you to speak of the estrangement's impact on your life. A counselor or therapist can take this a step further by introducing new coping skills that allow you to understand and adapt to your current situation.

For Friends and Community Members

Friends, colleagues, mentors, and community members may also be looking for guidance on how to best support a person in their social sphere who is estranged. Consider the following dos and don'ts.

DO

1. Encourage new holiday traditions like Friends-giving in lieu of traditional Thanksgiving.

2. Remain compassionate to triggers in conversations about family.
3. Respect their choice to be estranged.
4. Follow their lead on whether they want to talk about the estrangement or not.
5. See them as a whole person, not just estrangement.
6. Listen when they choose to talk about their family.
7. Encourage healthy, supportive relationships with others.

DON'T

1. Push them to attend family gatherings that would make them feel unsafe.
2. Argue with them to reconcile because "they might regret it!"
3. Assume the reasons for their estrangement.
4. Label them selfish, impulsive, or manipulative for choosing estrangement.
5. Shame them because "family comes first."
6. Attack the character of their estranged parent, thinking it's helpful.
7. Expect them to reconcile when estrangement may be permanent.

Each estrangement comes from unique and personal circumstances for both daughter and mother. It can't be emphasized enough how important it is to realize that the decision to be estranged isn't an easy one to make. As a support person, attempt to set aside your own thoughts or opinions on the matter, in order to be fully present and compassionate for the person who has chosen estrangement in support of their own safety, survival, or mental health. Check your biases at the door and ask what would help them most in this moment. If you stumble and offend them, apologize. You are human first and can make mistakes. Pay attention to their body language and ask for feedback on how you can remain a valued support to them in this difficult process. By being genuinely caring and curious about their experience, you are conveying an important message of connection in an otherwise stigmatized existence of estrangement.

Dating and Estrangement   **18**

HEALING AFTER ESTRANGEMENT CAN TAKE a variety of forms, including but not limited to healing attachment trauma and investing in healthy connections with others. Healing attachment trauma can involve trauma work in a therapy setting, or securely attaching to maternal or parental figures as well as romantic partners. One of the biggest challenges for adult daughters estranged from their mothers is learning to trust their own judgment. They continue to criticize their self-worth and value to others with questions like, "Am I good enough? Do I deserve to be loved unconditionally? Am I lovable as I am?" Let's talk about the ongoing fears adult daughters may have, related to building a life with romantic partners who learn of their estrangement from their mothers.

1. *What if I'm broken and not worthy of love, including love from a romantic partner?*

   As we've seen through the *Estrangement Energy Cycle*, women go through a challenging and vulnerable transformation in their estrangement from their mothers. They can have a fear of brokenness or defectiveness that could be addressed in therapy to support their move from powerless victimhood to empowered survivor. As Anderson (2018) names in her book *Difficult Mothers, Adult Daughters*, it's the story women tell themselves that either keeps them stuck in powerlessness *or* supports their growth toward self-love and empowered change. Attempting to rewrite their inner narrative can be a step toward believing they are worthy of love from others.

Kasey was learning to rewrite her inner narrative about being worthy of love through journaling and crafting her future TEDx talk. Instead of staying in what she called "her victim place," a headspace that spurred her to drown her emotions in alcohol, she wanted to embrace everything that her chosen word *survivor* represented within her mind, body, and spirit.

2. *What if I choose a dating partner who is like my mother?*

Although uncomfortable for some, it's known in psychology that we are attracted to what is familiar and comfortable, which can mean some characteristics of our parents can be found in our partners. This phenomenon isn't even restricted to healthy characteristics, just predictable ones. In fact, when interviewing women who've experienced repeated domestic violence by their partners, some have articulated that it feels less scary to stay with a person whom they can predict, rather than trying to start over with someone new. Newness in domestic violence can invite feelings of unpredictability and therefore feel more threatening to their safety. It's one of the reasons we hear the phrase "choosing the devil I know versus the devil I don't!" Although this isn't always a worry when engaging new dating partners, we can find ourselves drawn to characteristics or behaviors in partners that mirror our mothers'.

Keisha felt shocked and embarrassed when she discovered that her boyfriend had similar unhealthy behaviors to her mother. Keisha had found herself in months of denial after spotting warning signs earlier in the relationship and was determined to make things work when she found herself pregnant. It wasn't until after her son was born that she realized she couldn't subject her infant, her other children, or herself to her boyfriend's behaviors any longer. She realized that his alcohol consumption wasn't even the most challenging part; it was the fact that he felt he could put hands on her and push her, echoing Keisha's experience with her mom, that spurred Keisha to pursue a separation from him.

The mirroring of behaviors of our mothers in others isn't restricted to just dating partners either. Sometimes we find ourselves recreating patterns of conflict with folks who mimic our mothers, resulting in us subconsciously or consciously seeking a better or different outcome when we engage them.

Nina was no exception. Once she was promoted into a leadership role at her workplace, she began butting heads with a colleague who demonstrated disrespect and insubordination when given directives by Nina. Since the emotions seemed super-charged, I asked Nina if this person reminded her of anyone else in her life, making the emotions feel that much bigger. With this pointed question, Nina was able to recognize that the disrespect and hostility she was experiencing with this colleague mirrored her mother. Not only that, Nina was able to see that her stubbornness to win this person over came from a deeper place of wanting to prove she could have a different, better outcome than she did with her mother before their estrangement.

3. *What if my dating partner judges me, shames me, or attempts to convince me to reconcile?*

Dating partners, like other community members and support persons, may feel that their efforts to get a woman to reconcile with her mother are coming from a good place. However, these intentions only add to a woman's feelings of guilt, shame, and inadequacy because of the invalidation they feel in response to the partner suggesting that they reconcile. Most potential partners aren't going to receive the full story early in dating because of a woman's worry of being stigmatized or misunderstood. Therefore, it's important for dating partners to check their own goals, biases, and agendas at the door, holding space for a woman to disclose if and when she's ready, without stepping into a rescuer or fix-it role.

Regina was attracted to her spouse when they started dating because of his neutrality toward her estrangement from her mom. Instead of jumping in with opinions, he responded by saying he wanted her to be happy and healthy—a response Regina wasn't used to hearing from others. What Regina failed to realize at first was that her spouse chose to engage in a rescuer role instead. He swept her off her feet in a speedy courtship; they were married within a month so that he could provide her with a home and a family when she had none.

4. *What if they see the estrangement as my fault, believing that if I were healthier, this wouldn't have happened?*

Women who estrange from their mothers bear the brunt of negative assumptions and judgment for making the decision to separate. This could include a snap judgment of their character, including assumptions about their mental health or resiliency to handle the mother-daughter relationship in ways where estrangement wasn't needed. This viewpoint can be especially hurtful when experienced as unsolicited advice by strangers, such as suggesting family therapy or giving mother another chance. As one woman I spoke with put it, she feels exhausted every time she has to go into any amount of detail about her estrangement from her mom because she feels like she has to justify her decision to others and educate them on their misconceptions at the same time.

Kathryn knew too well that there were people in her life who believed her temper was the reason for her conflict with her mom and possible estrangement. After all, they could only see Kathryn's unbridled rage in the present, not the abuse of her past. Kathryn fought hard against professionals and family members who wanted to label her with mental health diagnoses that placed the blame of her mother-daughter relationship conflict solely on her shoulders. She resented the message that her mental health made her dysfunctional, and she wanted others to acknowledge that her rage, anxiety, and trauma responses were all tied to something much older and more painful than the *DSM-5* criteria she met at present.

Toni, as a self-identified people pleaser and perfectionist in the field of medicine, knew that she was holding herself to higher expectations than anyone else. It was easy for her to question her value in the face of her mother's neglect and untreated, chronic depression when Toni was young. Her therapeutic journey required self-compassion and new boundaries to release herself from continuing to carry the burden of mom Jan's happiness and devastating depression in adulthood. Eventually, Toni was able to acknowledge that she could not prevent Jan's depression, which absolved her of being held responsible for alleviating Jan's depression symptoms as well.

5. *What if they think my choice to not have children is because of the estrangement from my mother?*

In some cases, an adult woman may make the choice to not have children as the result of her estrangement from her mother. She may be fearful that she will pass on trauma, behaviors, or patterns of conflict, feeling powerless to stop them from being passed from one estranged generation to the next. We captured Charlotte's estrangement response of wishing to embody superior parenting earlier in this book, including her unyielding determination that she would be nothing like her mother when parenting her own children. This is the other side of the coin. Some women will choose to parent differently, and some women will choose to not have children at all. It's important to recognize that the decision to have children or not may be related to the estrangement or it may be based on other factors entirely.

Take Enid, for example. Upon finding things getting more serious with her boyfriend, she knew a conversation about children was inevitable. Although her boyfriend worried that the conflict among Enid, her mother, and her grandmother would influence her decision, Enid was quick to clarify that her biggest concern about having children was the risk of passing on genes connected to addiction within her family. Through some serious grounding and plenty of water, Enid and her boyfriend were able to address their hopes and fears together, when exploring whether they wanted to embark on a journey into parenthood as part of their future as a couple.

In having some of the same fears of adult daughters listed above, the most common fear of dating partners relates to their value and permanency within the relationship. They may have an inner voice asking if their partner could discard their family members—their blood relatives—through the act of estrangement, what's the possibility of them discarding the partner too? This can manifest as an anxious attachment relationship style that would require time, reassurance, and a secure attachment response to reduce their anxious presentation. The good news is that a healthy connection is possible for both an estranged woman and her dating partner. By connecting with healthy partners and relationships outside of their conflictual relationship with mother, our clients can find evidence that they are worthy of love and acceptance just as they are.

Life After Estrangement

19

WOMEN WHO WORK THROUGH THEIR own *Estrangement Energy Cycle* find clarity and self-acceptance, recognizing their own worth and contributions in the world as they know it. Per Anderson (2018), it's the difference between honoring the facts of the mother-daughter relationship, and recognizing the story a daughter tells herself about her relationship with her mother. A negative story focused on powerlessness can keep an adult daughter feeling stuck, whereas a story of estrangement that honors her choices to put her mental health and physical well-being first can have an empowered feeling that keeps her moving forward in her own healing journey. This positive shift in a woman's perceptions of her own value can oftentimes take years and should be normalized as having both moments of momentum and moments of stagnation.

Healing from estrangement does not have a one-size-fits-all approach because it revolves around matters of the heart and complex emotions, making it appropriate for a therapeutic setting. I have been honored to work with dozens of brave women over the years who wanted something better for themselves, their families, and their children. Estrangement isn't synonymous with happily ever after; however, there have been some amazing things to witness as a mental health professional, when women do the hard work estrangement energy requires. I'm happy to share what life after estrangement looks like for our nine adult daughters featured throughout this book, in celebration of their efforts to have healthy relationships and self-acceptance with or without mom.

Kasey successfully abstained from alcohol, even after her mother died. She recently celebrated three years of sobriety within her recovery community and allowed herself to fully feel the entire spectrum of emotions that came with it, trusting her community to handle her display of emotion in ways her family couldn't. Kasey is halfway through writing a book on her experiences and is in the process of applying to give her dream TEDx talk on the lessons she's learned. She reports she continues to visualize taking her place on that red dot on stage in order to help others through her story. Kasey emailed me to share that she was asked to lead a mentorship program in sobriety. When she inquired as to why she was selected, the staff shared that her community had nominated her because of her authenticity, compassion, and support of others as a committed sponsor and community member. She reports she can't wait to get started.

By learning to accept accolades and compliments from colleagues with grace, Toni was offered her dream job in medicine at a new clinic in her area. She and her spouse have reconnected in having the house to themselves, thanks to Jan investing in resources to maintain her mental health, allowing her to celebrate being free from depression for almost a year. Toni continues to challenge her former people-pleasing habits by saying no to projects and distractions that aren't in alignment with her current goals. She's pursuing mentorship of medical students in the hopes of helping them find work-life balance before they finish school.

Kathryn is on year six of holidays at home and continues to invite her chosen family and friends to meals when it feels good to her. She has learned that she can change her plans when needed to prevent fatigue and resentment too. When we last worked together, she was considering letting her teenage daughter go see her grandma for a week on her own. At her therapy closing session, Kathryn celebrated that she had regained the ability to laugh again instead of the near constant rage. She also acknowledged that she still has a temper at times and continues to use her coping skills to manage it. With plans to pursue the occasional cathartic release for her anger, she is in the process of recruiting folks for a scream therapy group she wants to start at her yoga studio, in order to help herself and others continue to express anger in healthy ways.

Enid is talking about future wedding plans with her boyfriend after celebrating two years together and recently getting engaged. Although her mom still struggles with substance abuse and ongoing addiction, she and Enid's grandma are respecting Enid's boundaries, including not making demands on Enid's time or giving unsolicited advice about her relationship or mental health needs. Enid feels more present and close to her boyfriend after facing her former avoidance head-on to work through her childhood trauma. Thanks to having clear boundaries with the most important people in her life, Enid's panic attacks are few and far between. She sees panic's unwanted return in her life as an indicator to revisit her boundaries, checking for warning signs of overdoing things or having some aspect of her life feel out of balance. It's a valuable skill she's taking away from therapy to help her navigate future milestones that may have stress attached to them, including wedding planning between two excited and opinionated families.

Charlotte and her mom, Sandra, are six months into healing and are taking it slow as they attempt to repair their relationship. Charlotte has gone as far as to have her kids meet Sandra a couple of times. Each encounter comes without any expectation of them having a long-lasting, trusting relationship because of Charlotte's current cautious state with Sandra. Although slow going, Sandra sees their shift in dynamic as progress, hoping she can build a meaningful relationship with her daughter and grandchildren over time. In the meantime, Charlotte continues to monitor her occasional desire to be a superior parent, gently challenging her own aspirations to eliminate perfectionism. She continues to question her motives when she attempts to take on something big. By remaining curious about what's driving her decisions, Charlotte has been able to slow down and be more present for herself and others, including each of her kids.

Nina has overhauled her entire life, cultivating a lifestyle that includes remaining sober, happy, and in a committed, healthy relationship. She no longer feels that heaviness in her belly that she had previously self-medicated with drugs or food. She has come to accept her body as she's aged, rejecting her mother's critical voice in her head for an inner voice that is gentler and more understanding. Currently, Nina is advancing in her career through several promotions, which offer her the opportunity to develop her leadership skills and practice having a voice in matters that are important to her. Although she continues to experience a significant number of trauma anniversaries each year, she is proud of her ability to handle them in ways that support her goal of feeling in control. Her progress over the years has made her a huge advocate for mental health therapy, reengaging in her own therapy sessions as needed when new challenges arise.

After a few significant roadblocks, Regina has found some success in building maternal connections with community members she can trust. She and her spouse went to several couples counseling sessions to address negative patterns of conflict and avoidance within their relationship. This has allowed them both to feel heard while practicing healthy communication skills and remaining emotionally regulated. Regina has set boundaries with extended family, including a request that they not speak to her of her mother, stepfather, or brother in honor of her current estrangements. By freeing herself of the stress and dysfunction she'd experienced before completing her trauma therapy, Regina has been able to get pregnant with her first child.

Keisha eventually came to a place of acceptance regarding the estrangement from her mom, Jeanie. She has not regretted her choice to separate from her boyfriend, electing to raise her three kids on her own as a single mom instead. Keisha has built herself a community of support through other moms in her neighborhood and has discovered a love for interior decorating, refurbishing old furniture, and organizing small spaces. Not only does she believe that the organization within a home leads to a healthier mindset; her skills in these areas have evolved into a lucrative small business where Keisha gets to be her own boss.

Summer was recruited to spearhead a new school program based on her specialty of working with at-risk children. Although she reports she's as busy as ever, her anxiety has become more manageable in having passion projects to focus on. Summer's ability to self-regulate is helping her daughter to flourish socially and academically, and Summer finds herself considering a relationship with her younger sister after several years of polite distance. Summer's greatest skill for maintaining her mental health is to ask herself, "is this productivity or busyness?" By slowing herself down with this question, Summer continues to make more intentional choices about projects or tasks she could take on within her life, keeping her relationship with her daughter as her top priority.

A Final Look at Estrangement Energy 20

Estrangement is not the goal of mother-daughter relationships—or any parent-child relationship for that matter. Yet clinicians are seeing more women work on themselves in therapy to address relationship concerns and conflict, including trauma, abuse, and neglect. When these negative childhood or adult experiences are present, and healing is absent or stagnant with mom, relationship rupture is a real possibility. Should the abuse continue or if mom is unwilling or incapable of contributing to the healing process for her daughter, estrangement becomes an option, however difficult it may be. This response serves to protect the mental health of adult women in taking back their power.

As community members, our number one goal is to access abundant compassion when encountering a woman who's exploring estrangement from her mother. To remain mindful of the possible negative impact of conversations about family and to understand the triggers that come with holidays and trauma anniversaries. To recognize how estrangement involves grief and loss with no guarantee of acceptance or closure that can come with time for other significant losses. To embrace questions like "who's really important in your life?" rather than "tell me about your family." To encourage women to find support and do work around the painful experience of estrangement, so they don't have to go through this alone.

As mental health professionals, there are dozens of clinical tools to assist clients on their journey, whether their final destination be estrangement or reconciliation. It is our responsibility to meet our clients where they are, offering a safe space to do this deep, oftentimes painful work. With our support, women can successfully navigate the *Estrangement Energy Cycle*, coming out the other side with tools for healing, new identity formation, and the ability to thrive in the present, with or without a healthy mother-daughter relationship. This is the gift they give themselves and their future daughters, where estrangement may be a necessary step to grow into the resilient women they were always capable of being.

Appendix A
Warning Signs in the
Mother–Daughter Relationship

WARNING SIGNS IN THE MOTHER-DAUGHTER RELATIONSHIP

WARNING SIGNS FOR DAUGHTERS

	Please mark the most applicable response to each question	NEVER	SOMETIMES	OFTEN	ALWAYS
1	You agree to things for your mom that violate your own boundaries to avoid a conflict.				
2	You feel responsible for your mother's happiness or mental health.				
3	Your emotions are dismissed, minimized, or ignored by your mother.				
4	You recall a childhood where your mother was absent.				
5	You remember having to make your own food or attend to your own needs from a young age.				
6	You feel like you make decisions about your life, career, or relationships to please your mom.				
7	You feel emotionally drained after long visits with your mother.				
8	When you see your mother's name on the caller ID, you feel anxiety or dread.				
9	You are drawn to fun-loving or affectionate mom characters in movies.				
10	You feel like your efforts are never good enough for your mom.				

WARNING SIGNS FOR MOTHERS

	Please mark the most applicable response to each question	NEVER	SOMETIMES	OFTEN	ALWAYS
1	You frequently ask your daughter for help.				
2	You expect your daughter to attend to your needs similar to a partner or spouse.				
3	You have passed on anxieties and fears to your daughter.				
4	You have shared intimate or personal details with your daughter as a confidant.				
5	You worry that you are passing on negative patterns of behavior to your daughter.				
6	You are concerned that you messed up or weren't around enough during your daughter's childhood.				
7	You put relationships like a new dating partner as a higher priority than your daughter when she was a child.				
8	You struggle with your emotions or mental health.				
9	You struggle with substance use.				
10	You feel detached and numb in your relationships, including your relationship with your daughter.				

estrangementenergycycle.com | © Croswaite Counseling, PLLC, 2022

Figure A.1. Warning Signs in the Mother-Daughter Relationship

Appendix B
The Estrangement Energy Cycle

Estrangement Energy Cycle

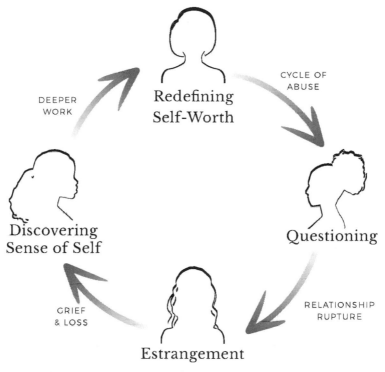

Figure B.1.   The Estrangement Energy Cycle

Appendix C
Estrangement Energy Therapeutic Tools

Download the handouts at estrangementenergycycle.com.

EXERCISE 7.1. **Negative Core Beliefs Tree**

Step 1: Grab a piece of paper or download our handout at estrange mentenergycycle.com. Self-worth is deeply rooted in beliefs we carry based on the earliest experiences we have in life. To make these beliefs more approachable to self-discovery, let's use a tree visual. Draw a picture of a tree with leaves, trunk, and roots or download our handout for a tree template.

Step 2: The worries and anxieties we are consciously aware of are the leaves of the tree. These are the things we can easily verbalize such as stressors and concerns. Things like "I'm always late. I feel like a bad friend. I'm always running late. I don't stand up for myself." What are your worries and anxieties related to your relationship with your mom? Write them in the leaves of the tree.

Step 3: Going deeper cognitively, we ask ourselves what these thoughts say about us, which gets us to the trunk of our tree. We may recognize thoughts like, "I'm lazy. I'm a slacker. I'm a bad friend." Write down key phrases or thoughts on the trunk of your tree.

Step 4: We continue to ask ourselves the question, "if this is true about me, what does this say about me?" to go even deeper, in order to get to the roots of the tree. The roots represent the negative core beliefs that drive our behaviors and can feel painful to explore—negative core beliefs like "I am unlovable. I'm a failure. I'm unworthy." Capture your negative core beliefs in the roots of your tree.

Step 5: Now that you are aware of your negative core beliefs, what would you prefer to believe? Write the opposite of your negative core beliefs or another, more positive belief to the side of your tree. Make sure it's an "I" statement! Try on statements like "I am lovable as I am. I'm trying the best I can. I am worthy." Which are easier to embrace or accept?

EXERCISE 7.2. **Dialectical Behavioral Therapy (DBT) Wise Mind**

Step 1: Draw a Venn Diagram or download our handout at estrange mentenergycycle.com. Label the left circle "logic" and the right circle "emotion."

Step 2: When thinking about your relationship with your mother, what emotions show up? List them in the **emotion** circle (e.g., sadness, anger, outrage, shock, denial, grief).

Step 3: When thinking about your relationship with your mother, what dynamics or facts can you name that are grounded in **logic**? List them in the logic circle (e.g., my mom is depressed, my mom has her own trauma, she's lashing out, I am the child of an emotionally immature parent, this mistreatment is a form of abuse, I want this pattern to stop, we can repair, this can get better).

Step 4: **Wise Mind** is the intersection of emotion and logic. When you hold space in your mind for both your emotions and logic, what do you hear or see? What needs to happen to support your autonomy in the mother-daughter relationship? What are your next steps to remain grounded and in control of your own actions? Write these in the intersection of your Venn Diagram that is Wise Mind.

EXERCISE 9.1. **Inner Critic Personification**

Step 1: Have a piece of paper and pen nearby or download our handout at estrangementenergycycle.com. Get into a comfortable position and close your eyes or put them at rest (e.g., looking down and softening your gaze). When you bring your attention inward and allow yourself to feel your inner critic, what does it look like? What represents it best, a person or an object? How do you feel toward it? Write down what you are noticing.

Step 2: Now that you know your inner critic, can you talk to it as if it's a separate entity to help reduce its power? Notice when it likes to show up. What it says to you. What do you want to say to it now that you are feeling more separate from it? Write down some things you can say.

Step 3: Picture a container in your mind to hold your inner critic now that you know it better. Visualize placing it in the container, focusing on the container size, material, and shape. Once your inner critic is successfully inside the container, visualize sealing it and placing it somewhere safe to allow your mind, body, and emotions to regulate. Note your container size, shape, and location on your piece of paper for future reference.

EXERCISE 9.2. **Letter of Divorce**

Step 1: Grab a piece of paper or download our handout at estrange mentenergycycle.com. A letter of divorce signifies a separation in a relationship that originates in substance abuse and recovery work, specifically divorcing your addiction. Rather than being exclusively used for this purpose, consider what you would write to your mom related to the stressors or strain in your relationship. Jot some things down.

Step 2: Allow yourself to write freely and with full emotion. Avoid self-censoring as this writing is for your eyes only. What are you noticing? What themes are coming up that are worthwhile to note or to continue to work on at a deeper level? Note the themes on your piece of paper.

Step 3: Read your divorce letter out loud, recognizing how it makes you feel to hear in your own voice.

Step 4: To honor the difficult and vulnerable work you've just done, what is the next appropriate step? Do you want to hold onto this letter as part of your work? Would you benefit from releasing yourself from it, such as tearing it up or burning it? Do what makes you feel most comfortable. Remember, you can write as many drafts or letters as you need to, to fully express yourself.

EXERCISE 9.3. **Cognitive Behavioral Therapy (CBT) Best–Worst–Most Likely**

Step 1: Grab a piece of paper or download our handout at estrange mentenergycycle.com. When thinking about your relationship with your mother, identify a scenario you've been contemplating such as confronting, allowing a relationship with your children, reconnecting, disconnecting, or inviting her to the holidays.

Step 2: What comes to mind as the best-case outcome in your scenario? Write it down.

Step 3: What comes to mind as the worst-case outcome in your scenario? Write it down.

Step 4: What comes to mind as the most likely outcome in your scenario? Write it down.

Step 5: Reread your responses to best, worst, and most likely scenarios and sit with any emotions that come up. How does this influence your decision? Based on what you've discovered, where do you go from here?

EXERCISE 9.4. **Trauma Family Tree**

Step 1: Grab a piece of paper or download our handout at estrange mentenergycycle.com. Start by mapping out your family tree, with you in the middle and noting partner/spouse, children, parents, grandparents, and extended family if appropriate and desired.

Step 2: Indicate the level of connection between you and each family member. A solid line indicates a connection. A double solid line indicates closeness in the relationship. A dashed line indicates a relationship that is now distant such as divorce, separation, or estrangement. A broken line indicates no relationship of any kind.

Step 3: Write down key facts that you are aware of about each person next to their name. Note things like age, occupation, mental health history, substance use history, abuse history, and fighting style.

Step 4: What trends do you see, if any, related to the key factors listed above? Is there a theme of helping professionals in the family? A string of divorces? A common fighting style of yelling or avoiding? Mental health of anxiety and depression present from generation to generation? Abuse cycles from grandparent to parent to child? Estrangement in multiple relationships or generations within the family tree?

Step 5: Further notice what emotions and sensations arise for you as you look at your family tree. What emotions do you feel? What clarity can this exercise bring you at this stage in your life? What cycles or patterns do you wish to break in your generation or your children's generation?

EXERCISE 9.5. **5-4-3-2-1**
*(Grab the script and an audio file
for download at estrangementenergycycle.com.)*

Step 1: Take note of your surroundings and begin with three belly breaths.

Step 2: What are 5 things that are blue (or any color you pick)? Name them in your mind or out loud.

Step 3: What are 4 things you can hear? Name them in your mind or out loud.

Step 4: What are 3 things you can touch? Name them in your mind or out loud.

Step 5: What are 2 things you can smell? Name them in your mind or out loud.

Step 6: What is 1 thing you can taste? Name it in your mind or out loud.

The five senses can be in any order. Notice how your mind calms in having a task that prevents rumination on other, more stressful topics. Repeat this exercise as many times as needed!

EXERCISE 9.6. **Thought-Stopping Technique**
*(Grab the script and an audio file for download
at estrangementenergycycle.com.)*

Step 1: Identify a negative thought that you are having in this moment.

Step 2: Ask yourself, what is the evidence of the thought being true?

Step 3: Ask yourself, what is the evidence of the thought being false?

Step 4: Ask yourself, is this a fact or feeling?

Step 5: Ask yourself, why am I having this feeling? What was the trigger?

Step 6: Ask yourself, what am I going to do now with these feelings?

EXERCISE 9.7.   **Watch Your Warning Signs**

Step 1: Grab a piece of paper or download our handout at estrange mentenergycycle.com. Draw four quadrants. For the top two boxes, write "Physical" in one box and "Psychological" in the other. For the left side of the quadrants, label one "Wellness" and one "Decline."

Step 2: Write the physical symptoms you recognize in yourself for Physical Wellness in the appropriate box. Write the physical symptoms you recognize in yourself for Physical Decline in the appropriate box.

Step 3: Write the psychological symptoms you recognize in yourself for Psychological Wellness in the appropriate box. Write the psychological symptoms you recognize in yourself for Psychological Decline in the appropriate box. Note if any of the decline warning signs are present for you in this time of your life.

Step 4: Next, draw a second 4-box quadrant for self-care or download our handout at estrangementenergycycle.com. For the top two boxes, write "Quiet" and "Active." For the left side of the quadrants, label one "Together" and the other "Alone."

Step 5: Write self-care ideas that are quiet and together in the appropriate box. Write self-care strategies that are active and together in the appropriate box.

Step 6: Write self-care strategies for quiet and alone in the appropriate box. Write self-care ideas that are active and alone in the appropriate box.

Step 7: Check your calendar. Where can you schedule self-care each week? Which of these self-care options can you implement right away versus planning ahead for them in your calendar?

EXERCISE 9.8. **Eye Movement Desensitization and Reprocessing (EMDR) Resource List**

Step 1: Grab a piece of paper or download our handout at estrange mentenergycycle.com. On your paper, draw a table that is two boxes wide and three boxes long for a total of six boxes. Label each of the boxes: (1) Supports/People (2) Things/Habits/Behaviors (3) Beliefs/Thoughts (4) Self-Soothing (5) Safe/Helpful/Positive Places (6) Active/Passive Coping

Step 2: Fill out examples in each box that are applicable to you. If you get stuck, ask a loved one or someone who knows you really well what they see that calms you under stress. This can add insight and ideas to your worksheet. The goal is to have multiple possibilities for positive coping in each box when responding to trauma or stress symptoms.

Step 3: Gather any tangible items you've identified in your resource list to keep at the ready. For example, perhaps you have a fidget tool on your keyring, have built a playlist of songs that elevate your mood, or keep mints or essential oils in your bag to help ground you.

EXERCISE 9.9. **Five Senses Coping Kit**

Step 1: Grab a piece of paper or download our handout at estrange mentenergycycle.com. Write down the five senses across your paper as See, Smell, Taste, Touch, and Hear.

Step 2: Reflect on what images calm you when you are upset or stressed. Write down ideas under the "See" column.

Step 3: Reflect on what smells bring you comfort. Write down ideas under the "Smell" column.

Step 4: Reflect on what tastes are nostalgic or comforting to you. Write them down under the "Taste" column.

Step 5: Reflect on what things you like to touch that bring you comfort. Are they smooth? Soft? Warm or cold? Write down ideas under the "Touch" column.

Step 6: Reflect on things you can hear that are comforting—things like nature sounds or music. Write down ideas under the "Hear" column.

Step 7: Now that you've identified a list of possible comforting items for your five senses, begin to collect those items or keep them handy for use in stressful moments.

EXERCISE 11.1.   **Successful Self-Visualization**

Step 1: Grab a piece of paper or download our handout at estrange mentenergycycle.com. Read through this script before following the steps as we encourage you to do this exercise with your eyes closed.

Step 2: The script:

Get into a comfortable position and take three deep breaths.

Clear your mind, imagining you are in a dark, calm room.

Begin to imagine an image of yourself, an image of success.

What do you look like in this room? How is your posture? What are you wearing? What is your face doing?

Allow the image to pan out in your mind's eye. Who is around you? What is around you in this image of success?

What are you feeling as you see this image of yourself?

Allow yourself to feel positive sensations throughout your body as you continue to breathe.

Take a snapshot—like on your phone—of this image in your mind's eye. What *word* would bring this image back into focus within your mind at another time?

Say that word out loud. How does it feel?

Write the word down.

EXERCISE 11.2.   **Trauma Personification**

Step 1: Have a piece of paper and pen nearby or download our handout at estrangementenergycycle.com. Get into a comfortable position and close your eyes or put them at rest (e.g., looking down). Bring your attention inward and allow yourself to get curious about your trauma. What piece feels most distressing? What sensations are associated with it? What imagery? What name or phrase captures the trauma element or event? Write down what you are noticing.

Step 2: When you are ready to contain the trauma between moments of reflection or therapeutic work, visualize a container. Visualize placing it in the container, focusing on the container size, material, and shape. Once your trauma personification is successfully inside the container, visualize sealing it and placing it somewhere safe to allow your mind, body, and emotions to regulate. Note your container location on your piece of paper for future reference.

EXERCISE 11.3. **Who Am I Reflection**

Step 1: Grab a piece of paper or download our handout at estrange mentenergycycle.com. By drawing lines, cut the piece of paper into four (4) quadrants. In the top left quadrant, write "I am." In the top right quadrant, write "I want." In the bottom left quadrant, write "My blocks," and in the bottom right quadrant, write "My solutions."

Step 2: Fill out each box with what comes to mind. Ask yourself questions like, "What are my roles? What adjectives describe me? What do I want from my relationships, my career, and my personal life? What is blocking me from achieving my goals? What are my possible solutions to rid myself of these blocks?"

Step 3: Notice any themes within the quadrants or any emotions that show up in completing this exercise. If you are still struggling with answers to your blocks and solutions boxes, who can support you in making progress?

EXERCISE 11.4. **Self-Portrait Exercise**

Step 1: Grab a blank piece of paper or download our handout at estrangementenergycycle.com. Begin by sketching out a head and torso for your self-portrait. Artistry is not the goal here so don't let your perfectionism get the best of you!

Step 2: Inside the torso of your drawing, write words that describe the roles you hold (e.g., wife, mother, daughter, artist, employee, volunteer).

Step 3: Inside the head of your drawing, write words that describe any anxieties and worries you have, such as your relationship with your mother, your productivity, your abilities as a parent, burnout, depression, or being overworked.

Step 4: Around the outside of the torso in your drawing, write words to describe you including your physical features, values, personality characteristics, and adjectives as desired.

Step 5: Around the outside of the head in your drawing, write words that capture what you need from others, such as compassion, understanding, space, hugs, distraction, affection, time to yourself, or reassurance.

Step 6: Review the final self-portrait, exploring key words that stand out or hold the most power over you in this moment. Grab some colored pencils, crayons, or colored pens and shade in the torso and head if you like. Focus on shading your drawing from left to right for bilateral stimulation and deeper processing as you continue your reflection of who you are and how you show up in the world.

EXERCISE 11.5. **Compassionate Touch Exercise**

Step 1: Grab a piece of paper or download our handout at estrange mentenergycycle.com. Begin by getting into a relaxed and present position, most likely seated, with feet flat on the floor and hands placed gently in your lap. Take several deep breaths.

Step 2: Begin an experiment with touch, starting with your dominant hand on neutral parts of your body. This might mean clasping your other hand, touching your feet, or resting your hands on your knees. Notice any sensation that arises from this touch.

Step 3: Continue exploration of compassionate touch, including holding your arms in a self-hug; touching your face, the top of your head, or the back of your neck; or placing your hands over your heart. Make note of which touch feels most comforting or evokes feelings of warmth for you. Also note which touch is not a good fit in feeling charged or uncomfortable.

Step 4: Recall a criticism or stressor and make note of any uncomfortable sensations in your body. Engage in your chosen compassionate touch as you continue to recall a criticism or stressor. Notice how your body and mind respond to the compassionate touch in the face of anxiety or worry, reinforcing any alleviated sensations or movement toward warmth and relaxation due to the compassionate touch.

EXERCISE 11.6. **Power Poses (Courtesy of Amy Cuddy)**

Step 1: Grab the script and an audio file for download at estrange mentenergycycle.com. Select a flat surface free of obstacles for standing or modify the poses for a sitting position if desired.

Step 2: Select one of three power poses below. Hold your selected power pose for at least two minutes. Breathe deeply and notice your strength and balance in this pose. Hold this power pose for as long as you feel comfortable.

Power Pose #1 V for Victory

Stand with your feet shoulder-width apart and raise your arms into a V position above your head. Keep your shoulders down and breathe through your belly, inhaling through your nose, exhaling out your mouth.

Power Pose #2 Wonder Woman Pose

Stand with your feet shoulder-width apart and put your fists on your hips. Feel your chest open up and breathe through your belly by inhaling in through your nose, exhaling out your mouth.

Power Pose #3 Open Pose

Stand with your feet shoulder-width apart and bring your hands up, elbows at your waist. Your hands will be palm up like an open yoga pose. Breathe through your belly by inhaling through your nose, exhaling out your mouth.

EXERCISE 11.7.　**Mindful Walking**

Step 1: Grab the script and an audio file for download at estrange mentenergycycle.com. Select a flat surface free of obstacles for walking, either indoors or outdoors.

Step 2: Take several deep breaths as you straighten your spine, imagining a pole coming out the crown of your head that elongates your neck, spine, and torso. Take several more deep breaths, noticing any shift in your breathing by adopting this upright posture.

Step 3: Begin to notice your feet. As you prepare to lift one foot to begin walking, become aware of your muscles shifting, balancing the movement of your body weight as you lift your foot.

Step 4: As you proceed to lift one foot to begin walking, embrace an exaggerated slowness, as if you are moving in slow motion. Without losing your balance, notice the muscle groups that activate as you begin to walk, including the lifting of your foot, bending of your knee, balancing on one foot, and placing your foot on the ground in a stepping motion, heel to toe.

Step 5: Repeat these slow-motion movements as you walk, noticing how your body uses muscle and balance as it moves. Continue your walking with relaxed belly breaths and a straight, strong spine.

Step 6: As you finish your mindful walking, what do you notice in yourself? Is there a burst of energy? Increased oxygen? An improved flow to your breathing?

EXERCISE 11.8.   **Wellness Recovery Action Plan (WRAP)**

Step 1: Grab a piece of paper or download our handout at estrange mentenergycycle.com. Create a table that is two boxes wide and four boxes long. Label the top left box "What does it look like when I'm well?" Label the top right box "What does it look like when I'm not well?" For the second row, label the left box "Warning Signs/Internal" and label the right box "Triggers/External." For the third row, label the left box "My Supports" and the right box "When things are breaking down." For the final row, label the left box "Plan of Action" and the right box "What do I need from others?"

Step 2: Fill out the boxes to the best of your ability as they relate to you and your experience. If you get stuck, you can ask someone close to you like a loved one or spouse about how you show up when feeling well versus unwell. We've also included some common responses from others in our handout available for download for further reflection.

Step 3: Share your discoveries about yourself with someone who can hold you accountable, specifically focusing on "Plan of Action" and "What do I need from others?" sections. The WRAP plan is meant to help you identify signs of decline and burnout while creating a path and plan toward wellness.

EXERCISE 11.9.   **Safe Space**

Step 1: Grab the script and an audio file for download at estrange mentenergycycle.com. Get into a relaxed position with your feet flat on the floor if sitting. Close your eyes or put them at rest, softening your gaze.

Step 2: Take several deep breaths as you allow yourself to relax and bring your attention inward. Begin to bring to mind an image of a place that feels safe. This place can be real or imagined.

Step 3: Focus on this safe space in all its detail. What are the sounds of this place? What can you smell? What can you taste, touch, and see?

Step 4: Notice how you feel in this space. If it begins to feel like anything other than relaxed, calm, happy, or safe, you may need to restart this exercise to identify another safe space.

Step 5: Once you have your safe space captured in vivid detail, choose one word that would represent this space, giving you access to it again in your mind. Try out the word by saying it in your mind or aloud. If it feels positive and reinforces the imagery of your safe space, write the word down.

EXERCISE 12.1. **Thought Diffusion**

(Grab the script and an audio file for download at estrangementenergycycle.com.)

The script:

Step 1: Identify a negative thought about yourself.

Step 2: Identify the sensation in the body this thought creates.

Step 3: Say out loud: the negative thought.

Step 4: Say out loud: "I'm having the thought that . . ."

Step 5: Say out loud: "I'm noticing I'm having the thought that . . ."

EXERCISE 12.2. **Container Exercise**

Step 1: Grab the script and an audio file for download at estrangementenergycycle.com. Get into a relaxed position with your feet flat on the floor if sitting. Close your eyes or put them at rest, softening your gaze.

Step 2: Take several deep breaths as you allow yourself to relax and bring your attention inward. Identify all the things you wish to contain, things that are upsetting or require containment in not feeling safe to process in this moment. These things may be represented as objects, words, or images.

Step 3: Imagine a container to put these items in. Focus on the size, shape, color, and texture of the container. Visualize placing each item in the container, one by one.

Step 4: Check that all the desired items are successfully in the container. Visualize sealing the container and identify a safe place to store it, either real or imagined. Complete the visualization by seeing the container in this safe place.

Exercise 12.3.   **Internal Family Systems (IFS)
Self-Meditation**

Step 1: Grab the script and an audio file for download at estrange mentenergycycle.com.

Step 2: Read the script from start to finish before attempting, or play the audio file; you will want to keep your eyes closed or at rest for this exercise.

Script:

Get into a relaxed position and take several deep breaths.
Close your eyes and go inside . . .
And begin by focusing on your body sensations . . .
Just noticing wherever your attention goes in your body . . .
And being in that sensation.

Whether it's a warmth in your hands . . .
A tingling in your face . . .
A pressure in your belly . . .
Or a tension in your shoulders . . .
Whatever it is, just be present with that sensation.

As time goes on, your attention may wander.
Bring it back to your body.
Even a different part of your body . . .
And allow yourself to be present with that sensation.

As you focus on your body, allow it to relax you . . . and take you deeper inside yourself.
Just continuing to be with your body . . . deepening into yourself.

And now focus your attention on your belly, the sensations in your belly.
Whether it's a fullness . . . or a softness . . . or a solidness . . .
Or just the rise and fall of your belly with each breath . . .

Whatever it is, just be present with the sensations in your belly . . .
And allow them to take you into that place in your inner awareness . . .
Anchoring you . . . in your belly . . . coming to a grounded, solid place inside yourself.

Exercise 14.1. **Emotional Freedom Technique (EFT) Tapping**

Step 1: Download the diagram of tapping points at estrangement energycycle.com.

The total list of tapping points are

1. The heel of your hand
2. Your inner eyebrow
3. Your temple
4. The place where your undereye meets your cheekbone
5. The skin between your nose and your lip
6. The skin between your chin and your lip
7. Your collarbone
8. Your lowest rib at your side
9. The top of your head

Step 2: Identify any negative or charged sensations in your body as you recall your worries or stressors. Begin by tapping the heel of your hand with your opposite hand. Name out loud your worries or stressors, without censoring, reframing, or revising your word choice.

Step 3: Move down the list of tapping points as you express your emotions out loud. Allow your worries or thoughts to come to you as you tap.

Step 4: Complete three or more cycles of tapping as you move down the tapping points on your body. Notice any shifts in the negative sensations that were present at the beginning of the exercise. Notice which tapping spots you found most comforting or liked best. Repeat your tapping cycle as needed for the desired positive shift in sensations and emotions.

Appendix D
Estrangement Clinical Competencies and Self-Assessment

ESTRANGEMENT CLINICAL COMPETENCIES AND SELF-ASSESSMENT

Name _____ Date of **Assessment** _____

ASSESSMENT				
Please mark the most applicable response to each question	NEVER	SOMETIMES	OFTEN	ALWAYS
1 Clearly asks about client relationships as part of case conceptualization.				
2 Effectively gathers information on client relationship dynamics as they relate to client's presenting concerns of estrangement.				
3 Identifies risk factors for estrangement from a trauma-informed perspective.				
4 Recognizes physical and emotional symptoms connected to estrangement energy.				
5 Identifies the client's current stage within *The Estrangement Energy Cycle*.				
6 Develops treatment goals that are appropriate for the client's current stage of estrangement.				
7 Remains knowledgeable about when to seek additional information from the client for added context and conceptualization.				
8 Incorporates cultural considerations from the RESPECTFUL Model.				

PROFESSIONALISM				
Please mark the most applicable response to each question	NEVER	SOMETIMES	OFTEN	ALWAYS
9 Maintains appropriate boundaries with clients.				
10 Remains aware of own biases and beliefs related to the family system and estrangement.				
11 Offers abundant compassion and zero judgment.				
12 Adopts client preferred language for estrangement experience.				
13 Avoids advice-giving or recommendations to reconcile or estrange.				
14 Identifies countertransference and seeks support when necessary.				
15 Pursues additional education, consultation, or supervision when needed.				

INTERVENTION				
Please mark the most applicable response to each question	NEVER	SOMETIMES	OFTEN	ALWAYS
16 Forms a collaborative, working relationship with the client which includes rapport.				
17 Provides psychoeducation on attachment, trauma, and estrangement as appropriate.				
18 Identifies different therapeutic tools congruent with the client's current stage of *The Estrangement Energy Cycle*.				
19 Adapts therapeutic interventions to be culturally relevant and compatible for client work.				
20 Requests feedback from the client on the therapeutic process to support goal progression.				

estrangementenergycycle.com | © Croswaite Counseling, PLLC, 2022

Figure D.1. Estrangement Clinical Competencies and Self-Assessment

Appendix E
Group Processing Questions

For Therapeutic Groups

1. Where do you find yourself within the *Estrangement Energy Cycle*? Why do you find yourself there?
2. Which woman do you relate to most in this book and why?
3. What therapeutic skill are you most eager to try in your own estrangement experience?
4. What do you want others to better understand about your estrangement?
5. What's one thing that can help you progress through the *Estrangement Energy Cycle*?
6. What do you need from others during your process?
7. How has your identity shifted in response to estrangement?
8. If you've been telling yourself a painful story about estrangement, what's the story you prefer to believe now, as part of your transformation?

For Book Club Discussion

1. Which woman's story in this book do you relate to most and why?
2. What is a key takeaway for you from this book?
3. What's one thing you can do to support others who are estranged or who are considering estrangement?

4. What therapeutic skill from the book do you find most helpful or applicable to your life right now?

5. If you've been telling yourself a painful story about your estrangement, what's the story you prefer to believe now, as part of your transformation?

References

Agllias, K. (2016). *Family estrangement: A matter of perspective* (1st ed.). Routledge.

Ainsworth, S. M. D., Blehar, M. C., Waters, E., & Wall, S. N. (2015). *Patterns of attachment: A psychological study of the strange situation* (Psychology Press & Routledge Classic Editions, 1st ed.). Psychology Press.

Anderson, K. C. L. (2018). *Difficult mothers, adult daughters: A guide for separation, liberation & inspiration.* Mango Publishing Group.

Ask Amy: Estrangement from family is hard to describe. (2022, August 11). *Arizona Daily Star.* https://tucson.com/lifestyles/ask-amy-estrangement-from-family -is-hard-to-describe/article_e00de73e-1420-11ed-892e-2715214d825e .html

Black, C. (1990). *Double duty: Dual dynamics within the chemically dependent home.* Ballantine Books.

Castro Croy, A. (2022). *Not my chicken* [Conference presentation]. TEDx Cherry Creek. https://www.ted.com/talks/alex_castro_croy_not_my_chicken

Centers for Disease Control and Prevention (2021). "Adverse Childhood Experiences (ACEs)." https://www.cdc.gov/violenceprevention/aces/index.html

Coleman, J. (2021). *Rules of estrangement: Why adult children cut ties and how to heal the conflict.* Harmony.

Cron, I. M. (2016). *The road back to you: An enneagram journey to self-discovery.* InterVarsity Press.

Croswaite Brindle, K. (2021). *Helpers with Hashimoto's: The rise of thyroid conditions in helping professionals and what we can do about it.* Croswaite.

Cukor, G. (Director). (1944). *Gaslight* [Film]. Metro-Goldwyn-Mayer. https:// www.imdb.com/title/tt0036855/

Gibson, L. C. (2015). *Adult children of emotionally immature parents: How to heal from distant, rejecting, or self-involved parents* (1st ed.). New Harbinger.

Harlow, H. F., Dodsworth, R. O., & Harlow, M. K. (1965). Total social isolation in monkeys. *Proceedings of the National Academy of Sciences of the*

United States of America, 54(1): 90–97. https://www.ncbi.nlm.nih.gov/pmc/articles/PMC285801/pdf/pnas00159-0105.pdf

Ivey, A. E., D'Andrea, M., Ivey, M. B., & Simek-Morgan, L. (2001). *Theories of counseling and psychotherapy: A multicultural perspective* (5th ed.). Allyn & Bacon.

Kübler-Ross, E., Kessler, D., & Shriver, M. (2014). *On grief and grieving: Finding the meaning of grief through the five stages of loss.* Scribner.

Levine, A. (2012). *Attached.* TarcherPerigee.

McBride, Karyl. (2008). *Will I ever be good enough? Healing the daughters of narcissistic mothers.* Atria Paperback.

McGregor, Sheri. (2016). *Done with the crying: Help and healing for mothers of estranged adult children.* Sowing Creek Press.

McMillan, D. (2022, July 25). *The badger and the turtle: A story to help your relationship* [Video]. YouTube. https://www.youtube.com/watch?v=G0mTtDTW9es

Merz, E. C., & McCall, R. B. (2010). Behavior problems in children adopted from psychosocially depriving institutions. *Journal of Abnormal Child Psychology, 38*(4), 459–470. https://www.ncbi.nlm.nih.gov/pmc/articles/PMC2892211/pdf/nihms198560.pdf

Tatkin, S. (2012). *Wired for love: How understanding your partner's brain can help you defuse conflicts and spark intimacy.* New Harbinger.

Waters, S. (2019). *Estrangement of parents by their adult children* (Rev. 2nd ed.). Sharon Waters.

Wolynn, M. (2017). *It didn't start with you: How inherited family trauma shapes who we are and how to end the cycle.* Penguin Books.

Index

About the Author

Khara Croswaite Brindle is a licensed mental health therapist and group practice owner in Denver, Colorado. She holds various roles including financial therapist, TEDx speaker, burnout consultant, published author, and professor. Khara values working with fellow mental health professionals through training, consultation, and clinical supervision, with her greatest joy being her work with driven entrepreneurs, fellow helpers, and perfectionists to help them move from workaholic to well balanced with streamlined strategies that fit their busy lifestyles. Khara is originally from the Pacific Northwest and gets her best ideas when walking outside and being around water. When she's not writing her next book or supporting fellow professional helpers on their own self-discovery journeys, she's playing with her daughter or indulging in gluttonous, gluten-free desserts with her family.